Twayne's Filmmakers Series

Warren French
EDITOR

George Cukor

George Cukor with author Gene Phillips on the set of Rich and Famous *(1981).*

George Cukor

GENE D. PHILLIPS

Loyola University of Chicago

BOSTON

Twayne Publishers

1982

George Cukor

is first published in 1982 by Twayne Publishers,
A Division of G. K. Hall & Co.

Copyright © 1982 by G. K. Hall & Co.

All photos courtesy of George Cukor's private collection.

Printed on permanent/durable acid-free paper and bound
in the United States of America

First Printing, July 1982

Library of Congress Cataloging in Publication Data

Phillips, Gene D.
George Cukor.

(Twayne's theatrical arts series)
Bibliography: pp. 183–86
Filmography: pp. 187–205
Includes index.
1. Cukor, George Dewey, 1899–
I. Title. II. Series.
PN1998.A3C87   791.43'0233'0924   82-899
ISBN 0-8057-9286-4   AACR2

This book is for James Welsh,
film scholar and educator

*The younger generation of directors still hasn't
learned some things about film making that
George Cukor forgot in 1911.*
                                        —Billy Wilder

Contents

About the Author

Gene D. Phillips, S.J., has known George Cukor since 1971 when they met just before the director began work on *Travels with My Aunt* (1972). Since that first interview, the author has met and interviewed the director several more times and maintained a correspondence with him as well.

The author is an elected member of the Society for Cinema Studies and teaches fiction and film at Loyola University of Chicago. He received the doctorate in English from Fordham University in New York City and has been chosen to serve on special juries at the Cannes, Berlin, Chicago, and Midwest Film Festivals. He has published more than seventy articles on literature and the film, and is a contributing editor for *Literature/Film Quarterly,* as well as an advisory editor for *American Classic Screen.*

His books include *The Movie Makers: Artists in an Industry; Evelyn Waugh's Officers, Gentlemen, and Rogues: The Fact Behind His Fiction; Stanley Kubrick: A Film Odyssey; The Films of Tennessee Williams; Hemingway and Film;* and *Ken Russell* and *John Schlesinger* for this series. He has contributed essays to such books as *Sexuality and the Movies; Ingmar Bergman: Essays in Criticism; Science Fiction Films; Graham Greene: A Collection of Critical Essays;* and *Contemporary Literary Scene, Second Series.*

Editor's Foreword

From the inception of this series, I never questioned that it must include a book about George Cukor; yet others wondered why. He had done his best-known work under the studio system when the director had little control over his choice of vehicles or his cast. He has never transcended the system by identifying himself with a particular film genre and making his name "above the title" a household word as Frank Capra had with his populist comedies of the 1930s, Cecil B. DeMille had with his biblical and patriotic spectacles, and John Ford had with his Westerns. Cukor never had the "final cut" all important to the auteurist director that would have given him complete artistic control over the release print of the film. (This account, in fact, frequently laments the way in which some of Cukor's best efforts were marred by producers' cuts.) Yet Cukor's record is remarkable. Not only is he the oldest person ever to direct a Hollywood feature film, but also all but one of the forty-nine preceding films for which he was principally responsible remain in circulation today.

Fortunately, on this occasion, I need not argue the case for Cukor as *auteur*, for this gratifyingly challenging task has been more capably and knowingly undertaken by Cukor's longtime friend, author Gene Phillips, in his own Preface. Yet it is appropriate to add here to Phillips's citations from Cukor, another relevant one from an interview that the veteran director granted the Fellows of the American Film Institute during a seminar in 1977. Asked about his working relationship with legendary actresses, Cukor responded: "The director has to know how much to say and when to shut up and what influence he has. They have to respect you, and they have to believe what you say. Then, too, you have to have a grip on the whole film, and you have to deliver the goods" (*American Film*, February 1978, p. 34). "A grip on the whole film"—the line that separates the competent craftsman from the immortal artist has probably never been more firmly and succinctly drawn.

Yet, even after these explanations, a question lingers—"a grip on the whole film" to what end? What indeed are "the goods" (in several senses of the word) that Cukor delivers?

Phillips finds a thematic unity in Cukor's films in his "predilection for depicting the collision of fact and fantasy in people's lives," especially in the lives of show people. While this insight cannot be gainsaid, it does not sufficiently distinguish Cukor from his professional colleagues, for the collision of fact and fantasy has been the principal business of the drama from *A Midsummer Night's Dream* to *Death of a Salesman*; and it has been even more often the burden of well-intentioned failures than of dazzling successes like Cukor's major films from *What Price Hollywood?* to *My Fair Lady*.

The "dazzling" qualities of these films provide the clue to understanding Cukor's unique career. The consistency of his work is not generic or thematic; it is stylistic. Of all the elements of Cukor's films focused on in this book, what one remembers most vividly about a Cukor film is the very quality that should make a film memorable— what it *looks like*. My own dreams continue after ten years to be influenced by the gorgeous flower garden and exotic railroad station of *Travels with My Aunt*, though this delight may be dismissed as one of Cukor's "less substantial" works. Similarly I remain one of the scattered staunch admirers of *Justine*, for whatever sins the producers committed in boiling Laurence Durrell's "Alexandria Quartette" down into a single, stunted movement, Cukor provided a visual equivalent for the novelist's florid prose.

Style, however, is too vague a term to pinpoint an author's genius, for everyone has a style however inadequate. Also, while Cukor has achieved more consistent control of a style than most film artists, there are other masters, like Renoir and Fellini and Nicholas Roeg, whose hypnotic styles could never be mistaken for Cukor's. The haunting question remains—style of what kind, and to what end?

The answer came to me one night after I had finished reading this affectionate account with rapt attention. I had the rare good fortune to be able to reinforce my untrustworthy memories of Cukor's work by revisiting for the first time in forty years the world of Marguerite Gauthier and her admirers and detractors in Cukor's *Camille*. I had the further good fortune to make this trip back to the mythical 1840s and 1930s in the exactly appropriate setting of the recently restored turn-of-the-century Claremont, New Hampshire, Opera House, which had earlier played host to many of the nineteenth-century's tear-jerking melodramas.

The only word that can be used to describe that evening's experience is one that was worked to death in the Hollywood of the 1930s but is rarely heard today—*glamorous*. Whatever else distinguishes the films that leap most immediately to mind as Cukor's work—*The Royal Family of Broadway* (though he was only partially responsible), *Dinner at Eight, David Copperfield, The Women, Born Yesterday,* the Judy Garland *A Star is Born*—they *are* glamorous.

Webster's well defines "glamour"—"a romantic, exciting, and often illusory attractiveness," something that film has a unique capacity to create. Looked at soberly, *Camille* is a piece of nonsense. Especially as sanitized to meet the demands of the Hays Office code, the jerkily episodic story line has little credibility; but what Garbo's Camille did was to overwhelm by enchanting the vision and transport the Depression-oppressed moviegoers of the 1930s into a fabulously realized world of furs, silks, and champagne, only to make them recognize at the end that such romance and excitement were indeed doomed illusions. The film allowed the spectator both to escape momentarily from his or her own dowdy world and then return somewhat reconciled to it. I am not sure that film can serve any more valuable function.

What is distinctive about Cukor's work is that it has been unfailingly glamorous (who else might crown his old age with a film called *Rich and Famous?*). Except for the handful of films that Josef von Sternberg made with Marlene Dietrich in the 1930s, no Hollywood studio films achieved so well as Cukor's what nearly everyone in Hollywood was trying to achieve in the 1930s and 1940s. As tastes have turned to violence, Cukor's films have become less central; but they continued to offer occasional refuges for those who preferred the lush old dreams.

What amounts to a consecration to glamour accounts, I think, for some of Cukor's most often cited qualities—the common association of his name with legendary actresses, his gentleness and courtesy in a neurotic community noted for temper tantrums and feuds, the seeming agelessness that he shares with a precious few like Lillian Gish and Gloria Swanson. The sociologist Hortense Powdermaker called her book about Hollywood "The Dream Factory." What distinguishes George Cukor is that of all the products of this manufactory, his have most consistently captured and preserved the most elusive of all commodities—dreams.

W. F.

Preface:
The Entertainer

The premise of this study of George Cukor, like that of my earlier volumes for this series on Ken Russell and John Schlesinger, is that the director alone can and must confer artistic unity on a motion picture. The director, after all, is the single controlling influence during the production of a film; hence it is up to him to blend all of the varied contributions of cast and crew into a unified whole. It is the director, consequently, more than anyone else involved in the making of a movie, who leaves his personal stamp on the finished product.

The proposition that the director is the center of the filmmaking process can be readily applied to European directors working in relatively small industries such as those in Sweden or France, where they can with relative ease control every aspect of the production of a film from beginning to end. At first glance, however, it seems much less apparent that an American director like George Cukor working in a much larger and more complex industry could gain a similar artistic control over his films.

On closer examination, however, it is clear that Cukor has been able with a fair degree of consistency to give his movies the imprint of his own personal vision and style in much the same fashion as his European colleagues have done, regardless of the diversity of genres in which he has worked. Indeed, one suspects that the "factory system" in Hollywood studios presented him with a challenge to his artistic creativity which sharpened his determination to turn out a succession of films over the years that he could in a real sense call his own.

Cukor has constantly sought to choose material that was congenial to his personal interests and talents. Hence he has succeeded in creating a world on film that is no less uniquely his own because he has created it with the aid of a host of collaborators.

"I don't say that I personally write or edit a picture," he told me recently; "but I do try to influence everyone that works with me on a film in order to get the best out of them that they have to give." For example, he goes over the script with the writer "scene by scene and line by line" before he goes on to the studio floor to shoot a motion picture. "I see what every individual working on the film can accomplish on their own, and then I make suggestions; and together we work out each step of the production. I let each of them know that I need every scrap of assistance they can give me."

Perhaps Cukor best explained his attitude toward the collaborative nature of moviemaking in an essay that he penned more than forty years ago for a book called *Behind the Screen*. "I want to make not only the stars but the assistant electricians feel that they are there to supply something to the composite whole of the finished picture that nobody else can supply," he wrote, adding that he is most pleased when the resulting film shows no visible signs of "direction" at all, because he as director has integrated as smoothly as possible into the completed movie the contributions of everyone associated with the production.

Since Cukor has directed fifty films—all but one of which remain in circulation at the time of writing—the customary plan in this series of a chronological film-by-film analysis of the director's career would not prove satisfactory. Cukor's films have rather been grouped in five chapters discussing his most memorable achievements—film adaptations of stage plays, films with Katharine Hepburn and Spencer Tracy, films with other legendary actresses, film adaptations of classic and popular novels, and the musical films to which he turned late in his career to achieve some of his greatest successes.

Although most of Cukor's films are adaptations of preexisting novels or plays, the sum total of his motion pictures nevertheless reflects the provocative personal vision and directorial style of the man who made them all. As Cukor himself explains, "If you select material that attracts you and touches your imagination, as I have always tried to do, your own originality will come out in your handling of it—if you have any originality." Cukor, as the succeeding pages will strive to show, possesses a great deal of that commodity.

GENE D. PHILLIPS

Loyola University of Chicago

Acknowledgments

First of all, I am most grateful to George Cukor, who discussed his films with me and corresponded with me about his work over the last decade; allowed me to select illustrations for this book from his own enormous still collection; and gave me access to his personal archive of documentation on the making of his movies, including taped dialogues of himself talking with Katharine Hepburn and with others.

I would also like to single out the following people among those who have given me their assistance:

Novelist Graham Greene, director Fred Zinnemann, actress Olivia de Havilland, and Irving Thalberg, Jr., the son of producer Irving Thalberg and actress Norma Shearer, for sharing their recollections with me about Cukor. Irene Burns, Cukor's secretary for nearly forty years, Dan Woodruff, Cukor's aide, and Cukor's longtime friends Robert Rosterman of Twentieth Century–Fox and Martial Capbern, formerly of Loyola University of Chicago, all of whom have been helpful to me in all sorts of ways.

Research materials were made available to me by the following: Patrick Sheehan, David Parker, and Emily Sieger of the Motion Picture Section of the Library of Congress; James Powers of the American Film Institute; Robert Harris of Images Film Archive; and David Shepherd of the Directors Guild of America. I wish also to thank Robert Cushman and Anthony Slide of the Academy of Motion Picture Arts and Sciences for processing the Cukor stills for this volume; film scholar Leo Murray for his careful reading of the typescript; and Mary Ellen Hayes for collating the filmography.

Some material in this book appeared in a totally different form in the following publications:

Film Comment, copyright 1972 by Film Comment Publishing Corporation, and reprinted from *Film Comment*, Spring 1972, by per-

Chronology

1899	George Cukor born in New York City, July 7, to Victor and Helen Cukor.
1918	After graduation from De Witt Clinton High School and service in the Students Army Training Corps during World War I, he enters the theater as a stage manager.
1920–1929	Directs plays in summer stock in Rochester, New York, throughout this period, and on Broadway from 1925.
1929	Summoned to Hollywood with the advent of talking pictures, and serves as dialogue director on *River of Romance*.
1930	Acts as dialogue director on *All Quiet on the Western Front*. Codirects *Grumpy*, *The Virtuous Sin*, and *The Royal Family of Broadway*.
1931	Moves on to directing features on his own with *Tarnished Lady* and *Girls about Town*.
1932	Replaced by Ernst Lubistch on *One Hour with You*. Directs *What Price Hollywood?*; *A Bill of Divorcement*, the first of tem films with Katharine Hepburn; and *Rockabye*.
1933	*Our Betters; Dinner at Eight; Little Women*.
1935	*David Copperfield*.
1936	*Sylvia Scarlett; Romeo and Juliet*.
1937	*Camille*.
1938	*Holiday* (British titles: *Free to Live* or *Unconventional Linda*).
1939	*Zaza*. Replaced by Victor Fleming on *Gone With the Wind*. *The Women*.
1940	*Susan and God* (British title: *The Gay Mrs. Trexel*); *The Philadelphia Story*.
1941	*A Woman's Face; Two-Faced Woman*.
1942	*Her Cardboard Lover*.

1943　　　*Keeper of the Flame. Resistance and Ohm's Law* (a training film made while he was serving briefly in the Signal Corps).

1944　　　*Gaslight* (British title: *Murder in Thornton Square*); *Winged Victory.*

1947　　　*Desire Me* (partially reshot by Jack Conway, Mervyn LeRoy); *A Double Life.*

1949　　　*Edward My Son; Adam's Rib.*

1950　　　*A Life of Her Own; Born Yesterday.*

1951　　　*The Model and the Marriage Broker.*

1952　　　*The Marrying Kind; Pat and Mike.*

1953　　　*The Actress.*

1954　　　*It Should Happen to You; A Star Is Born*, his first musical.

1956　　　Returns to the stage for *The Chalk Garden*, his only theatrical production after 1929. *Bhowani Junction.*

1957　　　*Les Girls; Wild Is the Wind.*

1960　　　*Heller in Pink Tights*, his only Western; *Let's Make Love.* Finishes *Song Without End* for the deceased Charles Vidor.

1962　　　*The Chapman Report. Something's Got to Give* canceled when Marilyn Monroe can no longer work.

1964　　　*My Fair Lady* earns him the Directors Guild of America Award, as well as an Oscar for best director on his fifth nomination; the movie is named best picture of the year, the fifth Cukor film to be nominated in that category.

1969　　　*Justine.*

1972　　　*Travels with My Aunt.*

1975　　　*Love Among the Ruins* is first telecast March 6; it wins him a best director Emmy for his first TV movie.

1976　　　*The Blue Bird,* the first and so far the only Russian-American coproduction; receives an honorary degree as Doctor of Humane Letters from Loyola University of Chicago.

1978　　　Gala tribute by the Film Society of Lincoln Center of New York to his lifetime achievement in the cinema.

1979　　　*The Corn is Green,* his second TV film, is first telecast January 29. Feted by the Chicago Film Festival, which is dedicated to him this year.

1980　　　Portrayed by actor George Furth in the segment of the TV mini-series "Moviola" treating the making of *Gone With the Wind.*

1981   *Rich and Famous,* his fiftieth film as a director, made at the age of eighty-one, marking him as having the longest continuous career in movies and TV of any director ever. Recipient of the D. W. Griffith Award of the Directors Guild of America on March 14; the thirteenth director to receive the award since its inception in 1953.

1

Hollywood Immigrant: The Early Years

A ROLLS-ROYCE, GLEAMING IN THE LATE MORNING sun on a warm September day in 1973, pulled up to the curb on Sunset Boulevard in Hollywood, and the front door swung open. Behind the wheel was George Cukor, who had graciously offered to drive me to his legendary home in West Hollywood for one of the many interviews that I have had with him about his films in the last ten years. I had first talked with him some two years earlier, but this was the first time that I was making the trip to his home.

George Cukor's short stature belies his status as a giant among film directors, while his sprucely tailored way of dressing, urbane, gracious manner, and silver hair bespeak the elder statesman of the film industry that he has become after half a century of making movies. His favorite way of describing someone he admires is to say that the person is witty, modest, and intelligent. Cukor, too, one learns in conversing with him, is effortlessly and consistently all three.

His estate, it turned out, is as elegant and as tasteful as his motion pictures, and is richly endowed with memorabilia associated with the greats of Hollywood history with whom he has worked in his long career. There is, for example, the Punch and Judy stage used during the credits of his classic Tracy-Hepburn comedy *Adam's Rib* (1949). The Academy Award which he won for *My Fair Lady* (1964) is perched inconspicuously on a high shelf in his office, where it has been joined since my first visit to his home by his Emmy for his first TV film, *Love Among the Ruins* (1975). These and other awards easily go unnoticed by a visitor; a veteran like Cukor, after all, has no need for self-advertisement.

Combining what Cukor has told me about his early life on that occasion and on others over the years, one comes up with the following profile of his youth. He was born of Hungarian immigrant stock in New York City on July 7, 1899, to Victor and Helen Cukor. He and his

George Cukor, with Katharine Hepburn, reminisces about his early career at the Lincoln Center gala in his honor, 1978.

sister were the only grandchildren of the Cukor clan, and his family cherished the hope that he would follow the family tradition of entering the law. "But," Cukor recalls, "I was always stage struck, and wanted to pursue a career in the theater."

From the second balcony he saw all of the great theatrical luminaries of the day, and he would later recall these boyhood experiences in making a picture called *The Actress* (1953), which deals with a similarly stage-struck youngster. Some of the stars, like John and Ethel Barrymore, he would himself direct on stage and screen in the years to come. "I looked down my nose at movies when I was a kid," he remembers. "But still I would go regularly to the movies and see the latest Max Linder comedy or Griffith epic."

After graduating from De Witt Clinton High School, Cukor enlisted in the Students Army Training Corps, in which he served until the end of World War I. His professional career in the theater began in 1919 when he became assistant stage manager of the New York and Chicago companies of a popular play entitled *The Better 'Ole*. Cukor moved up eventually to stage managing several productions for the Selwyn and the Schubert organizations, and for other important Broadway producers.

He also gained invaluable experience by spending the summers between each New York theater season as resident director of the Lyceum Stock Company in Rochester, New York, a post he held from 1920 to 1928. During his tenure in Rochester he had the opportunity of directing Broadway stars like Billie Burke and Louis Calhern, and the feisty young director's spirited productions gained him nationwide attention in theatrical circles.

Bette Davis has still not gotten over the fact that Cukor dismissed her from the company. At the time she was a shy young girl with a baby face who simply was not suitable for the mature roles Cukor was casting, and Cukor reluctantly let her go. "Apparently this was a soul-searing experience for her," says Cukor, "since she has referred to this episode constantly in interviews over the years. Finally I said to her one day, 'For God's sake, Bette, we've all been fired, and very likely will be again before we're dead and buried; so stop going on about this!'"

In 1925 Cukor became associated with the Charles Frohman Organization, a prestigious Broadway production company. Frohman had long since gone down on the *Titanic* (and therefore did not hire Cukor personally, as Gary Carey suggests in his Cukor monograph). The company was now run by the eminent producer-director Gilbert

Miller, with whom Cukor continued a working relationship until his departure for Hollywood a few years later.

Cukor helped Miller direct Maugham's *The Constant Wife* with Ethel Barrymore in 1926, and on his own directed Laurette Taylor the following year in the out-of-town tryout of a bawdy French farce entitled *Her Cardboard Lover*, the only work which Cukor was ever to direct on both stage and screen. Miller replaced both the director and the star before bringing the play into New York; Cukor then went on to direct five Broadway shows in quick succession before heeding the call of Hollywood in 1929.

He has returned to the theater only once in the course of his subsequent career, in 1956, when he undertook the direction of Enid Bagnold's *The Chalk Garden*. Serious artistic disagreements developed while the play was on the road, however, between Cukor, on the one hand, and the playwright, producer Irene Mayer Selznick, and designer Cecil Beaton on the other. (Cukor would later work again with Beaton on the film of *My Fair Lady*.) "I was dealing with some strong-willed, not to say disagreeable people who weren't interested in a damned thing the director had to say," Cukor comments laconically. "Finally I left the show after it opened in Boston, and Albert Marre took the play on to Broadway. On the way back to New York from Boston I felt that I was being let out of reform school." After nearly three decades of working in pictures, Cukor found the theater a relatively small-scale, not to say penny-ante operation by comparison, and has never hankered to direct another stage production since that time.

The Dialogue Director

In any event, when the movies learned to talk, Cukor, like many other stage directors, was summoned to Hollywood to work in the film industry. In February 1929, Paramount engaged him as a dialogue director, a position specifically created at the time so that someone with theatrical experience like his could help out silent film directors not adept at coaching actors in speaking lines to make the transition to talking pictures more smoothly. When he arrived in Hollywood, Cukor recalls, some veteran directors of silent films were still absentmindedly referring to the dialogue in the screenplay as "titles"—as if the lines were still going to appear on the screen in printed form rather than be verbalized by the actors on the sound track!

"When I got to Hollywood the studios were all petrified about the coming of sound to motion pictures," he goes on. "Directors lost their heads and began to abandon everything that they had learned about camera movement in the silent days." Until noiseless cameras were developed, the camera was for the time being quarantined in a soundproof booth, so that its mechanical noises would not be picked up on the sound track. For this reason the director had to use a different stationary camera for long shots, medium shots, and close-ups, after the manner of live television shows some years later. Moreover, until the stages in the studio could be insulated, talkies had to be shot at night, so that noise coming from outside the sound stages all day long would not be picked up on the sound track.

Confusion reigned, says Cukor. The so-called sound technicians had been recruited from the ranks of shipboard radio operators who knew nothing about filmmaking; yet they were dictating to actors and directors alike. "But gradually the techniques of making sound films were perfected and everyone got used to them," Cukor concludes. "After all, as Lionel Barrymore quipped at the time, 'Human speech has been a success for thousands of years. There is no reason why talking pictures shouldn't work out.'"

The first film to which Cukor was assigned as dialogue director was *River of Romance* (1929), the screen adaptation of Booth Tarkington's *Magnolia*, directed by Richard Wallace and starring Buddy Rogers as a river gambler. "It was a lovely play which I had seen on the stage with Lionel Barrymore as the riverboat captain," says Cukor. "Bing Crosby later did it as a musical called *Mississippi* (1935), with W. C. Fields as the captain."

The producer and the director did not appreciate Tarkington's witty dialogue, and cut some of the best lines in the script in order to place more emphasis on the so-so plot. "They had no respect for the text," Cukor complains, "but being a man of the theater, I did. As the venerable stage actress Mrs. Fiske used to say, they were wrong-headedly placing a firm, firm emphasis on the wrong, wrong note."

Soon after he arrived at Paramount, Cukor made friends with David O. Selznick, who was at that time executive assistant to B. P. Schulberg, head of the studio. Sensing that Cukor would never get anywhere in pictures working on minor movies like *River of Romance*, Selznick suggested to Schulberg that Paramount loan Cukor to Universal as dialogue director on the distinguished World War I epic *All Quiet on the Western Front* (1930), which Lewis Milestone was about to direct. "I sold Schulberg on the great value to Cukor of was about to direct. "I sold Schulberg on the great value to Cukor of learning screen technique from as great a silent director as Milestone," Selznick has said. At the same time he pointed out to his good friend Lewis Milestone, who was making his second talkie, the advantage of having a man with Cukor's theatrical experience at his side.[1]

Before shooting commenced, Cukor collaborated on the dialogue of the screenplay with Maxwell Anderson, whose play *Gypsy* he had staged on Broadway only the year before, and Del Andrews, a talented film editor whom Cukor found particularly helpful in teaching him the technical side of movie making. "I knew how to direct actors, but I didn't know how to use a motion picture camera," Cukor explains. Andrews taught Cukor about such things as maintaining visual continuity from shot to shot and choosing camera angles; and Cukor continued to use him as a consultant on some of his first directorial efforts such as *Little Women* (1933).

"I filmed the actors' screen tests for *All Quiet* and staged the movie's intimate scenes," says Cukor, "for which I had to train Lew Ayres and the other young men playing German soldiers in delivering dialogue, since most of them had no experience in sound pictures. I consequently gained a reputation for being able to help inexperienced players." (In the years ahead Cukor would continue to vindicate this reputation by introducing such newcomers as Angela Lansbury, Judy Holliday, and Tony Perkins to the screen.)

Cukor would be the first to concede that the great power of the movie was largely due to Milestone's overall direction of the film. He was nevertheless nonplussed when Milestone advised him after the picture was finished that he did not feel that Cukor should receive a screen credit as dialogue director on the film, because he did not deem it appropriate to "divide" his directorial credit with someone else. Of course Cukor's contribution to the film became generally known later on, but Milestone successfully blocked Cukor from receiving any official screen credit for his work on *All Quiet*. "I was not even invited to the studio party at the end of shooting," says Cukor, "because my name had already been stricken from the film's list of credits. To this day I don't understand his behavior, since Milly has always been a very generous man."

Film historian David Parker suggests that Milestone canceled Cukor's screen credit on *All Quiet* because he felt the need to prove decisively that he could make it on his own in talking pictures in the wake of the failure of his earlier work in sound. Still, at the time Cukor very much needed whatever credits he could accumulate in order to establish himself in the film industry, and Milestone's action was therefore a real blow to him.

"In my time people have not always given me proper credit for what I have done," Cukor notes. "Perhaps that is why, for my part, I have always made it a point to render credit where credit is due. Not that I am particularly noble; I just believe that giving everyone credit for whatever contribution they have made to a film doesn't take anything away from the director, while it might be of some help to them."

Another aspiring film director, Fred Zinnemann (*High Noon*), worked as an extra in *All Quiet on the Western Front,* and subsequently served as an assistant to Cukor on *Camille* (1937). "Cukor very kindly asked me to help him with camera angles and visual concepts," Zinnemann recalls. "While it was a most interesting and valuable experience for me, I do not see how it could have been of much value to George."[2]

Observing Cukor's unfailing willingness to perfect his grasp of the technical intricacies of film making with the aid of individuals like Del Andrews and Fred Zinnemann, veteran director William C. De Mille remarked that Cukor was "one of the few stage directors who really set out to study the motion picture as an art in itself."[3] "I didn't go to night school, but I watched other filmmakers at work," Cukor says in response. "It took me three or four years to cotton on to screen directing after coming from the theater. In films, for example, you are working with the actors and the camera and the microphone in very close quarters, whereas in the theater the actors have to project to the back of the house. When making a movie, therefore, the director has to keep in mind that what is a good performance for the stage would be overacting on the screen."

The Codirector

When he returned to Paramount after the completion of *All Quiet,* Cukor took another step toward becoming an accomplished filmmaker when he was assigned to codirect three films. The first codirector with whom he worked was Cyril Gardner, an excellent film editor, whose function on the set was to insure that the footage Cukor shot could be assembled smoothly in the editing room. "He was a very nice man and knew a great deal about the camera," says Cukor. "In working with a codirector, I would rehearse a scene and then step back and ask my colleague how best the footage might be cut together by the editor." With this in mind, Cukor would make any necessary adjustments in his staging of the scene, and then it would be photographed under the supervision of his codirector. "Working with a codirector was a genuine collaboration," Cukor points out. "We respected each other and did not encroach on each other's turf, so we got along."

The first of two films which Cukor and Gardner made together was *Grumpy* (1930), a remake of a 1923 movie originally filmed by William De Mille (and not by his brother Cecil, as Allen Estrin suggests in his Cukor monograph), which in turn was derived from an old-fashioned English comedy-mystery. The title role of the ill-tempered retired lawyer was enacted by Cyril Maude, who had created the role on the New York stage in 1913. In the course of the film a precious diamond which the old man was guarding for his granddaughter's beau is stolen, and granddad turns amateur sleuth long enough to recover the jewel and foster the romance of the young lovers.

Cukor could not be expected to make much of this warmed-over material; nevertheless, as Allen Estrin notes, the film is not without interest as the work of a neophyte director finding his way. At a time when so many talking pictures were mere photographed stage plays, Cukor began this movie with an exterior shot actually filmed in the great outdoors.

Before doing a second film with Gardner, Cukor codirected *The Virtuous Sin* (1930) with Louis Gasnier, a hack director of silent serials like *The Perils of Pauline* and later of low-budget sound films like the camp favorite *Reefer Madness* (1938), who was not much help to Cukor in filming material that was even less compelling than *Grumpy*. *The Virtuous Sin* was derived from a creaky Hungarian melodrama set in Russia in 1914, in which Maria (Kay Francis) bribes her way into a brothel in order to prevail upon one of the customers, General Platoff (Walter Huston), to exempt her husband, a medical student, from active military service in exchange for her favors.

Although Cukor enjoyed working with Kay Francis and Walter Huston, he now thinks *The Virtuous Sin* a dreadfully dated movie, and once expressed the hope that none of the prints of the film had been preserved—a fate that has befallen more distinguished early motion pictures than this one. His wish has not been granted, however, since the film has been rescued from oblivion and is currently in 16-mm distribution.

In his program notes for a New York screening of the film, movie historian William K. Everson, usually fairly benign in his assessment of minor films by major directors, calls *The Virtuous Sin* one of the worst movies ever to be "rediscovered." Everson excoriates the film's slow pacing and some heavy-handed performances among the supporting cast, but adds that the polished camera work makes up for a lot, as does the handsome scenic design (although the brothel appears to be the size of the czar's Winter Palace).

There is at least one nifty visual metaphor worth noting. To foreshadow the sexual encounter which will climax Maria's seduction of the general, Cukor has the pair riding a seesaw in the garden outside the brothel. The plank jutting out between Platoff's legs, with Maria seated astride it at the other end, thus becomes a gigantic symbol of male potency, and demonstrates a level of sly sophistication absent elsewhere in the film.

Cukor's third film in a row as a codirector was once more done in tandem with Cyril Gardner, and this time Cukor really exhibited his potential as a screen director to much better advantage than his two previous pictures allowed him to do. The film was a screen adaptation of the popular play *The Royal Family* by George S. Kaufman and Edna Ferber, which Cukor had been asked to direct on the stage back in 1927 before he left Broadway for Hollywood. The movie version was entitled *The Royal Family of Broadway* so that film audiences would not assume that it dealt with some European monarchy, when in fact it was a thinly veiled satire on the Barrymores, with Ina Claire and Fredric March standing in for Ethel and John Barrymore under the names of Julia and Tony Cavendish.

March, who had been chosen for his role after he was spotted playing the part in the national company of the show when it came to Los Angeles, stole the picture with his bravura impersonation of John Barrymore. In March's best scene, Tony delivers a hilarious monologue about his disdain for working in pictures as he marches up the grand staircase of the Cavendish mansion for a shower, shedding his clothes along the way.

Cukor decided to introduce some intricate camera movement into this scene by having the camera follow Tony up the stairs and into the bathroom—no minor accomplishment in 1930 when camera cranes were still hand operated rather than electrically powered, as today. Moreover, the scene had to be carefully planned so that the crew could adroitly pull furniture out of the camera's path as it followed Tony's progress from bedroom to bathroom. Clearly Cukor was developing a sense of cinema that would serve him in good stead when he began directing on his own.

Henrietta Crossman, Fredric March, Mary Brian and Ina Claire in The Royal Family of Broadway, *a satire on the Barrymores which Cukor co-directed in 1930.*

Despite Cukor's efforts to liberate the movie from its stagebound script and despite the fine editing by another director-to-be, Edward Dmytryk (*Murder, My Sweet*), the movie was not a success. Thirty years later, when there was talk of a remake, Cukor took another look at the movie and figured out why. "It seemed to me too thin-blooded and very special," he says in retrospect, because the satire on both the theater and the talkies which punctuated the literate dialogue was perhaps too sophisticated for the mass audience to appreciate. When Fanny Cavendish (Henrietta Crossman), the matriarch of the clan, refers condescendingly to movies as "all singing, all dancing, all terrible," that line might have struck the funny bone of audiences on the eastern seaboard, but may well have offended the Depression-ridden moviegoing public across the country for whom the talkies were a source of solace.

The only other film on which Cukor shared the set with another director, in addition to the three which he codirected in 1930, was *One Hour with You* (1932). This situation developed as a curious happenstance after Cukor had already directed two features of his own and had started to direct this film by himself as well. It all came about when Ernst Lubitsch, the great German-born director, prepared to do a remake of his saucy silent comedy *The Marriage Circle* (1924) as a musical starring two of his favorite players, Maurice Chevalier and Jeanette MacDonald. Lubitsch supervised the pre-production planning of the film, but had to finish *The Man I Killed* (1932), a serious antiwar drama, before turning to *One Hour with You*. When the war picture ran over schedule, Cukor was brought in to direct the musical with Lubitsch staying on only as producer.

"I did the best I could," says Cukor stoically, "but I wasn't Lubitsch." It was unrealistic for the studio to expect a comparatively new director brought in at the last moment to create a film that would have been on a par with the work of a seasoned moviemaker like Lubitsch. "When Schulberg didn't like the rushes, I offered to go off the picture, but he told me to stick with it. Then, after I directed the movie alone for two weeks, Lubitsch finally finished shooting *The Man I Killed* and assumed the direction of *One Hour with You*; and I was demoted to acting as his assistant. It was humiliating for me to have to sit on the sound stage while he directed the picture, although from time to time he would let me shoot a scene according to his specific instructions while he went off to supervise the editing of *The Man I Killed*. I behaved as well as could be expected in these awkward circumstances; and years later when I was brought in to tidy up a picture codirected by Arthur Ripley and Joshua Logan entitled *I Met My Love Again* [1938] before it was released, I told Josh that I would make it as painless as possible for him and Arthur because of what I had endured on *One Hour with You*."

After *One Hour with You* was completed, Schulberg added insult to injury by telling Cukor that, because Lubitsch's name was big at the box office, Cukor would receive no directorial credit on the film at all. This was clearly unfair, since the young director had directed enough scenes in the film to be termed at least a codirector of the movie. Moreover, advance advertisements for the film had already proclaimed the picture an Ernst Lubitsch production directed by George Cukor. Fed up, Cukor threatened to sue Paramount if they denied him a just screen credit on the film. "I wanted out of my Paramount contract anyway," he recalls, "because David Selznick had already invited me to join him at RKO where he was now working as an executive. Part of the out-of-court settlement of the suit was that Paramount would let RKO take over my contract in exchange for my accepting a listing in the screen credits of *One Hour with You* not as

Tallulah Bankhead in the foreground, with Elizabeth Patterson as her mother in
Tarnished Lady *(1931), Cukor's first solo effort as a director.*

codirector but as dialogue director," a function Cukor had not actually
performed on a movie since *All Quiet on the Western Front* (1930).

Before Cukor got involved in *One Hour with You*, he had, as
mentioned, already directed two films in his own right, *Tarnished
Lady* and *Girls about Town*. The first of these projects was offered to
him when he was making *The Royal Family* at Paramount's Long
Island studios, and producer Walter Wanger came up with a script
which could serve as Cukor's maiden voyage as a full-fledged
director.

The Director: *Tarnished Lady* (1931)

Tarnished Lady (1931) was based on a story by Donald Ogden
Stewart, which the author had himself adapted to the screen for the
movie debut of Tallulah Bankhead. But the film was more noteworthy
in the long run because it was the first collaboration of Cukor with
Stewart, who was to lend his talents to several screenplays for Cukor
films over the years. Cukor's initial solo flight as a director was a satire
on the amorality of New York high society, presenting Bankhead as

Nancy Courtney, a temptress who marries rich Norman Cravath (Clive Brook) for his money. She eventually falls in love with him, however, and sticks by him even when he loses everything in the 1929 stock-market crash.

Stewart was always noted for his snappy dialogue, and Bankhead is at her best when she is matching quips with Phoebe Foster as Germaine Prentiss, Nancy's rival for Norman's affections. But when she is called upon by the screenplay to be lovesick and vulnerable, as in the scene in which Nancy discovers Norman is still seeing Phoebe, Bankhead is simply not authentic. Her personality was too hard and aggressive for film audiences to believe that there was a softer side to her nature, as more than one critic noted.

Tallulah Bankhead "was never as at home on the screen as she was on the stage, as a matter of fact. She was a gifted actress, and on the stage she was enormously animated," Cukor explains. "But she never developed a comparable screen presence. Dear Tallulah was just not naturally photogenic; her eyes seemed deadly opaque on film, and her face never looked radiant, even when she smiled. Nevertheless, she wanted above all else to be a movie queen, but she didn't have what it takes."

If Bankhead did not come off to good advantage in *Tarnished Lady*, New York City did. More than a decade before film critics were praising postwar European directors for their use of real locations in their movies, Cukor was doing extensive location work on *Tarnished Lady* around New York City, including scenes set at a Fifth Avenue church and on the terrace of an apartment.

The camera work is interesting throughout, particularly for an early talkie, starting with the opening shot of Nancy smoking a cigarette while inexplicably wearing a blindfold. It develops that she is testing various brands of cigarettes for an ad endorsement. It is a pity that the film as a whole does not live up to this inventive beginning; but Cukor had not yet hit his stride as a director, either with this film or his next.

Girls about Town (1931)

Girls about Town was based on a story by Zoë Akins, whose play *The Furies* Cukor had directed on Broadway in 1928. The plot of Cukor's second directorial effort resembles that of Akins's *The Greeks Had a Word for Them*, filmed the next year by director Lowell Sherman (who, by the way, would star in Cukor's *What Price Hol-*

lywood? the same year). In both cases the story centers on a group of gold diggers who specialize in dating wealthy men passing through town on business. In keeping with the Motion Picture Production Code adapted by the industry in 1930, however, there is no implication in either *Girls* or *Greeks* that the girls provide their escorts with anything more than an evening's genial companionship, even though their succession of sugar daddies reward them with handsome gifts.

"As a result," Cukor comments, "these girls seemed to exist in a kind of never-never land. Although Zoë Akins portrayed them as the high-class tarts that they really were, they were made to appear on the screen as virtuous young ladies rather than as sinners." To that extent, he jokes, *Girls about Town* might have been better titled "The Virtuous Sinners." Although Cukor did not of course endorse the absurdly strict regulations of the early Code concerning the treatment of sex in movies, he does feel that filmmakers now go to the opposite extreme. "I'm not prudish, but I think things have gone too far now, because sex has lost some of the mystery which it should have when portrayed on the screen."

In any event, two of the young ladies of the title are Wanda (Kay Francis) and Marie (Lilyan Tashman). Although Tashman had played largely unsympathetic roles prior to this film, Cukor was able to nudge a delightfully relaxed performance from her in the present movie that was better than any she ever had the chance to give again before her untimely death in 1934. As Marie awakens in the late afternoon to prepare for another night of carousing, she orders "a bromo seltzer and the evening paper" for her breakfast. With this single line of dialogue Tashman manages to sum up the whole mad whirl of Marie's giddy existence.

Some critics found the intrusion of a serious subplot, in which Wanda's ex-husband tries to blackmail her fiancé (Joel McCrae), at odds with the overall lighthearted tone of the picture. Cukor replies that Wanda's near loss of her sweetheart simply exemplifies the fact that "there is often a serious moment in a comedy involving misunderstanding and heartbreak." That does not keep the picture in question from being essentially a funny film.

It was high time that this enterprising young filmmaker was given better material on which to lavish his talents. With his move to RKO from Paramount, this would soon come to pass.

2

The Play's the Thing:
Drama on Film

BY THE TIME THAT CUKOR LEFT PARAMOUNT to join Selznick at RKO the pair had become close friends. Indeed, they were often mistaken for each other on the lot. This was curious because, despite their facial resemblance, Selznick was about six inches taller than Cukor. When the producer's mother complained to Cukor about the situation, the latter replied good naturedly, "It's all right, Mrs. Selznick; my mother doesn't like it either."

Cukor's association with RKO was a rewarding one, since he was given much more creative freedom there than he had enjoyed at Paramount. Because the studios turned more and more to the theater for story material after the introduction of sound, several of the subjects which Cukor tackled during this period were adaptations of stage plays. The prevailing tendency of filmmakers at this time was to make a film derived from a stage play into a virtual replica of the original theatrical production. These films thus relied heavily on the play's theatrical dialogue on the misguided assumption that, as long as pictures were talking, it did not matter if much of what was being said was worth listening to. Because the characters in these wordy movies seemed to be endlessly convening in the drawing room for tea, films of this kind were dubbed teacup dramas.

For his part, Cukor was aware that motion pictures by their very nature must appeal primarily to the eye rather than to the ear as plays do, and that hence moving pictures must not cease to move by degenerating into mere photographs of talking heads. As already noted, Cukor had tried to enliven *Grumpy* (1930), the very first film he codirected, by shooting some footage on location in order to exploit the greater flexibility which the movie medium enjoys over the theater; and he continued to open out spatially for the screen his

Cukor conferring with Jean Harlow between takes on Dinner at Eight. (*Cukor was often mistaken for David O. Selznick, producer of the film, who was at the time erroneously identified as being in this publicity still.*)

35

later adaptations of plays by shooting some scenes on location whenever possible.

Nevertheless, opening out a play for the screen must always be done judiciously, he points out. "On the one hand you can't just turn out a photographed stage play; on the other hand you can't rend the original property apart. If you don't preserve what was worthwhile in the original play when you create a different version of the material for the screen, you will suddenly find that you have nothing left. The trick is to subtly give the original play more movement on the screen than it had on the stage." In addition to shooting some exteriors on location, regularly moving back and forth between different playing areas will keep a film from becoming static, even if the areas covered happen to be various room within the same basic interior set—so long as the scene is shot from a variety of camera angles representing the different points of view of the various characters.

This chapter will seek to illustrate that, despite his theatrical antecedents, Cukor is very much a man of the cinema who knows how to use his camera with equal dexterity both indoors and outdoors, even when dealing with material from the stage. As Andrew Sarris has written, "Cukor is fully capable of exploiting exteriors when they serve his purposes." Yet, when his characters have to confront each other in closer quarters, "Cukor glides through his interiors without self-conscious reservations about what is 'cinematic' and what is not."[1]

Rockabye (1932)

Among Cukor's first films at RKO was *Rockabye* (1932) with Constance Bennett and Joel McCrea. Ironically, Cukor was asked to replace another director on this picture, just as Lubitsch had shortly before taken over *One Hour with You* (1932) from him. *Rockabye* had originally been filmed by George Fitzmaurice, a competent moviemaker who had in his time directed Valentino and Garbo. But *Rockabye* had previewed badly, and Cukor was asked to take over as director once the script was substantially rewritten. He had to accomplish the task of extensively reshooting the movie in about three weeks' time, and everyone was exhausted on the final day of shooting. "We had to prop poor Connie Bennett up against a door to do the last shot," Cukor remembers.

Rockabye belonged to the cycle of "confession films" which were enormously popular in the early 1930s (*Tarnished Lady* was another example). Constance Bennett starred in a number of these pictures, in which the heroine more often than not produced an illegitimate baby as the by-product of an illicit romance. In fact, there is an in-joke in her other Cukor film of 1932, *What Price Hollywood?*, in which the movie star played by Bennett inquires if she must have a baby in every film she makes. Still, as film historians Griffith and Mayer comment, "Miss Bennett's children came in handy for many plot purposes."[2]

In *Rockabye* Bennett plays Judy Carrol, a stage star with a child that was probably fathered by her former gangster lover, though she insists that the baby was adopted, presumably to keep the civil authorities from branding her an unfit mother. Cukor sought to keep alive the long dialogue scenes brought over from the play not only by breaking up a scene into separate shots, but also by a device called "cutting within the camera," whereby the director can impart visual variety to a scene by subtly shifting the actors' positions within the frame while the camera remains stationary.

In one key sequence Judy tells a sympathetic friend (Paul Lukas) of the official efforts to deprive her of her child while the pair are standing in the foreground of the shot. When she walks away from the camera to confer with the boy's governess, she diminishes in stature as she goes—a symbol of the way that she has been belittled by those who deem her unworthy to be a mother. Cukor thus smoothly shifts from a medium shot to a long shot without the need for either camera movement or editing. This technique of cutting within the camera is ideal for sound films, as Arthur Knight suggests, since repeated cuts in a tense scene of this sort could detract from the importance of key dialogue passages and lessen the emotional flow of the performances.

Our Betters (1933)

Cukor's last film at RKO starring Constance Bennett provided a welcome change of pace for them both, based as it was on a sophisticated play by Somerset Maugham, with whom Cukor had been associated in the theater. Cukor, of course, admired Maugham's work, but he had misgivings about whether or not *Our Betters* was really picture material. "It was a brilliant, cynical play," he explains; "but it was about a very special subject, one that the average moviegoer didn't know anything about: American women who marry British titles."

Pearl Grayston (Constance Bennett), an American heiress who has moved to England and married into the aristocracy, is as sleek and durable as the hardware that her wealthy family manufactures. She has wed Lord Grayston (Alan Mowbray) for his title, while the impecunious aristocrat, no less an opportunist than she, has married her for her fortune. Pearl and Grayston, quite obviously, deserve each other. He continues to maintain a mistress after their marriage, while she boasts a succession of lovers including Peppi (Gilbert Roland), an oily gigolo supposedly attached to Pearl's middle-aged friend Minnie (Violet Kemble-Cooper), who is now a duchess.

When Pearl's sister Bessie (Anita Louise) discovers Pearl and Peppi in compromising circumstances during the course of a weekend party at the Grayston country house, Pearl mollifies the jealous Minnie by sending for Ernest, a mincing dance instructor with painted, Kewpie doll lips, whose lessons are currently the rage among aging socialites like Minnie, to teach Minnie to tango. Minnie and Pearl accordingly are reconciled; but Bessie, permanently disenchanted with Pearl's decadent life-style, decides to return to America rather than become further involved with her sister's shallow, pseudosophisticated smart set.

Cukor's film of the Maugham play has been criticized for softening Pearl's character to make her more likable. "We didn't try to," Cukor replies. "She is still an unscrupulous woman in the picture. If movie audiences like her it is because she is also witty and charming." Indeed, one must grudgingly admire the slick, stylish resourcefulness which Pearl displays in manipulating and outwitting her fashionable friends. In the selfish, social-climbing world which Pearl inhabits, her victims usually get no more than what is coming to them, for Pearl is in reality only beating them at their own game.

Cukor makes two telling visual comments on Pearl's character in the course of the film. During a royal reception at Buckingham Palace, Pearl snatches from the floor a precious pearl that has been accidentally dropped by another guest. Though she returns it to its rightful owner, her first instinct is to swallow it, thereby showing the voracious, predatory side of her nature. At another point Minnie sardonically praises Pearl's virtue, and Cukor cuts immediately to a shot of Pearl on her way to her soon-to-be discovered assignation with Peppi.

Pearl is as polished as a glittering diamond, and just as hard and sharp-edged. She is manifestly proud of what she terms her "force of character, wit, unscrupulousness, and push." Constance Bennett is splendid as Pearl. "Poised, beautiful, calculating, she is a veritable queen bee around whom the others buzz in attendance," writes Jeffrey Richards.[3] In his deft direction of Bennett and the fine supporting cast headed by Violet Kemble-Cooper as Minnie, Cukor proved as never before his skill in handling high comedy.

Dinner at Eight (1933)

By this time Selznick had gone to Metro-Goldwyn-Mayer, where he set up his own production unit and once again asked Cukor to join him. For Cukor the move to Metro marked the beginning of an association with that studio which was to last for nearly a quarter of a century. Though he would be loaned out by MGM to direct films at other studios from time to time, the majority of his films during this period would be made at Metro.

The first Cukor-Selznick venture at MGM was the screen version of *Dinner at Eight* (1933), a comedy by George S. Kaufman and Edna Ferber, whose play *The Royal Family* Cukor had codirected as a film at Paramount three years before. In the earlier movie Fredric March had limned a hilarious impersonation of John Barrymore which reportedly had amused Barrymore very much. Now Cukor was directing the great actor himself.

John Barrymore was just one member of the stellar cast of *Dinner at Eight*, which also included his brother Lionel, Jean Harlow, Wallace Beery, and Marie Dressler. "Because I was working with such accomplished actors, I was able to shoot that picture in a little over twenty days," says Cukor; "and that fact was always held against me." That is to say that, thereafter, whenever Cukor complained that the shooting schedule of a picture was too short, Metro executive Eddie Mannix would invariably remind him that he had made *Dinner at Eight* in record time.

Jean Harlow was the least experienced of the stars in the expert cast, and Cukor worked with her very intensely in order to bring out the best that she had to offer. "When I first met her, Jean seemed to me to be just a shy girl dominated by her mother," Cukor recalls. "That she had been already typed as a wicked woman in the parts she played amuses me still. Before she made *Dinner at Eight* she had only been making pictures for two or three years, and she was still terribly self-conscious."

Cukor discovered in working with her, however, that she was a natural comedienne who could, like Marilyn Monroe many years later, deliver a double entendre as if she were blissfully unaware of the risqué implications of what she was saying. In *Dinner at Eight*

Harlow turned in the most sensational performance of her tragically short career (in four years she would be dead).

Although Cukor now quips that he must have had "a lot of damned nerve" to take on the high-powered ensemble of actors that he directed in the present film, he was not the least bit intimidated by them. "You must never be scared of the people you are working with," he explains. "They have to feel that you know what you are doing. If you are a director who they know can deliver the goods, they will respect you and be all for cooperating with you."

In *Dinner at Eight* Cukor gave full rein to the theme that was to characterize so much of his later work: the attempt of individuals to reconcile their cherished dreams with the harsh realities of their lives. Cukor has frequently explored this theme in terms of show people, since, more than anyone else, professional performers run the risk of allowing the world of illusion with which they are constantly involved to become their only reality. This theme had already surfaced in earlier Cukor films. For example, the family of troupers in *The Royal Family of Broadway* (1930) and the heroine of *Rockabye* (1932) are wedded to their fantasy world of the stage in a way that makes a shambles of their private lives; and, as we shall soon see, Larry Renault, the defeated and destitute former matinee idol in *Dinner at Eight*, is clearly cast in the same mold.

But Cukor's theme of the conflict of illusion and reality in people's lives reaches beyond Renault to encompass several other characters in the film as well. *Dinner at Eight* revolves around a dinner party being given by the social climbing Millicent Jordon (Billie Burke), who is unaware that the steamship business run by her husband Oliver (Lionel Barrymore) is on the rocks, and that Oliver himself is dying of a heart condition. As we meet each of the guests in their own personal milieu before they set off for the dinner party, we discover that each of them in turn is likewise nursing pretensions of one kind or another that are peculiarly their own.

Dan and Kitty Packard (Wallace Beery and Jean Harlow) are vulgar *nouveaux riches* who are trying to achieve a respectability that ill befits either of them, a situation that Cukor would further examine in *Born Yesterday* (1950). Larry Renault (John Barrymore) is a second-rate, hasbeen actor who has allowed a combination of false pride and alcoholism to ruin his career, but nevertheless gallantly insists that he can make a comeback—until he loses what he knows is his last chance for a decent part and decides to commit suicide.

Cukor recalls shooting the scene in which Renault ends his life. "I told Jack that since the actor had bungled everything in his life, something should go wrong even with his suicide, which the actor wanted to be very dramatic and tragic. As Jack walked across the room to plug up the chimney before turning on the gas, he tripped over a footstool and sprawled ignominiously on the floor. It was just the right pathetic touch."

There is another ironic detail in the death scene: just before Renault dies, he instinctively adjusts the lampshade near the chair in which he is to expire so that the light will properly illuminate his handsome profile. If Cukor is unsympathetic to the unreal dreams of wealth, fame, or respectability that so many of the characters in his films cherish, he nevertheless treats the dreamers themselves with compassion, as he does Renault, or at least with indulgent good humor, as he does the Packards.

By the time that the dinner party begins, one by one each of the central characters is made to face up to reality. Mrs. Jordon, for instance, recognizes the worthlessness of her aspirations for social preferment when she learns of her husband's illness and business crisis. When Kitty Packard meets Oliver Jordon, she realizes what a decent person he is, and blackmails her crooked husband into helping Jordon save his business instead of taking advantage of Jordon's financial plight, as Packard had originally intended to do.

Nevertheless Kitty, a former hatcheck girl, is not above continuing her dogged attempt to make a good impression on her social betters while talking with Carlotta Vance (Marie Dressler), a former actress who has gracefully accepted the eclipse of her career in a way that the proud Larry Renault could not. As they go into dinner, Kitty remarks to Carlotta, "I was reading a book the other day. It's all about civilization or something. Do you know that the guy said machinery is going to take the place of every profession?" Carlotta, by now slightly tipsy, responds with the film's now-famous closing line, "Oh my dear, that's something you need never worry about."

Romeo and Juliet (1936)

With *Dinner at Eight* Cukor at last hit his stride as a director of significance, and was now asked to direct other star-studded Metro productions like *Romeo and Juliet*. The basic drawback to Cukor's sensitive, intelligent rendering of Shakespeare's play is that—despite the fact that one publicity release for the film was headed "Boy Meets Girl: 1436"—the title roles were played by Leslie Howard and Norma Shearer, who were unfortunately a bit beyond the proper age to enact credibly Shakespeare's star-crossed young lovers.

Gary Carey has written that there is an abiding paradox about screen actors playing Shakespeare's youthful heroes and heroines: by the time an actor has gained the insight and experience needed to essay one of these roles, he has reached an age when the camera lens relentlessly reveals in every close-up a maturity that is out of keeping with the requirements of the role. That paradox holds true in the present instance.

Irving Thalberg, MGM production chief, had planned the picture as a vehicle for Shearer, who happened to be his wife. "He was ambitious for her," Cukor remembers; "but I think she was an extremely worthy actress. Some of the scenes in *Romeo and Juliet* I think Norma did with great power," such as the long take in which Juliet agonizes over carrying through her ruse to fake her death by taking a sleeping potion in order secretly to be reunited with Romeo, who has been banished for mortally wounding her kinsman Tybalt in a duel.

The performance of Leslie Howard, who was offered the role only after it had been passed up by Laurence Olivier, also has its moments, as when Romeo poisons himself at Juliet's grave on the tragic assumption that she is really dead. But Howard's Romeo by and large lacks the passion and fiery impetuosity called for by the part; and his portrayal of Hamlet in the Broadway production which he directed only a few months after the release of *Romeo and Juliet* was likewise criticized in some quarters as being too staid.

But Cukor was not crossed by the rest of the galaxy of stars in his cast, including Basil Rathbone as the vicious Tybalt and John Barrymore as Romeo's carefree sidekick Mercutio. Barrymore, the most experienced Shakespearean actor in the film, stands out in particular for his memorable delivery of Mercutio's celebrated spoken aria, the tongue-twisting "Queen Mab" speech. He imbues the speech with a lyrical lilt which makes it one of the finest Shakespearean vignettes ever committed to film.

Barrymore's performance more than repaid Cukor's efforts to keep him from being fired by Irving Thalberg when the actor's drinking problem began to interfere with his work. With tragic irony Barrymore was in real life beginning to resemble Larry Renault in *Dinner at Eight,* and Cukor was later to draw on his experiences with

Barrymore during the making of *Romeo and Juliet* in delineating the character of the alcoholic actor in *A Star Is Born* (1954).

"Jack Barrymore was a wonderful actor and a charming, intelligent fellow; and I enjoyed working with him very much," Cukor remarks. "It was tragic that he finally lost his grip on himself and became such a sad, sad creature. Irving was very long-suffering, and if he wanted to get rid of Jack on *Romeo and Juliet* it was only because he honestly thought that Jack was no longer capable of doing the film. But Jack worked hard and finished the picture."

Graham Greene commended the film in his review of the London opening for treating the mass audience to more of Shakespeare's words than filmgoers had grown to expect in Shakespeare movies. In fact Cukor contends that no significant liberties were taken with the text, and recalls in this connection the longstanding joke in the film colony about the Douglas Fairbanks–Mary Pickford 1929 talkie version of *The Taming of the Shrew*. An enormous amount of derision was heaped upon Sam Taylor, the hapless writer who did the screen adaptation of the play, because of the screen credit which proclaimed that the script for the film was by William Shakespeare "with additional dialogue by Sam Taylor."

There were no substantial alterations of any kind in the dialogue of Cukor's *Romeo and Juliet*, aside from some prudent pruning of the lengthy text, supervised by Shakespearean scholar William Strunk of Cornell University, for the sake of clarity. "The text of the play as filmed was absolutely pristine," says Cukor; "and anyone who thinks otherwise had better go back and read the play."

Greene did take the movie to task, however, for the excesses of its production design. Friar Lawrence's little cage of a cell with its "few flowers and weeds," writes Greene, becomes in the film an elaborate laboratory stocked with test tubes and beakers which make the good monk seem to be a scientist in some latter-day science-fiction film, rather than the modest botanist that he is. Juliet's balcony is so high above the ground, Greene continues, that logically the young lady "should really have conversed with Romeo in shouts like a sailor from the crow's nest sighting land." By contrast, it is the small, simply staged scenes, devoid of such opulent design, that come off best in the picture, Greene maintains: for example the scene between "Romeo and the ruined apothecary he bribes to sell him poison was exquisitely played and finely directed."[4]

Greene's point is that the film's ornate sets appear on occasion to be so cluttered as to distract the viewer from Shakespeare's richly evocative verse. The reason that the quality of the film's scenic design is uneven is that Cedric Gibbons, MGM's resident art director, constantly feuded with Oliver Messel, whom the studio had imported from the London theater to collaborate with him. Cukor now regrets that he was not more decisive in making Gibbons work with Messel instead of against him. "If I'd been more forceful," he concedes, "we'd have arrived at something better."[5]

Despite its drawbacks, however, *Romeo and Juliet* is a film of which the director can be justly proud. As already stated, the screenplay preserves intact most of Shakespeare's original text, and all of the players help to render it accessible to the average filmgoer by giving clear, sensible readings of the playwright's matchless poetry. What's more, Cukor's film is superior in this regard to the two subsequent Anglo-Italian film versions of the play directed by Renato Castellani (1954) and Franco Zeffirelli (1968). Zeffirelli, for example, amputates more than half of the original dialogue, including Juliet's stunning soliloquy about drinking the sleeping potion, which Norma Shearer delivered so superbly.

Yet Cukor's *Romeo and Juliet* is by no means mere canned theater. His cinematic sense is much in evidence throughout the film, especially in the way that his flexible camera unflinchingly records the violence of Romeo and Tybalt's duel and adroitly captures the splendor of the sumptuous masked ball, which looks like a Renaissance fresco come to life. Besides being more popular than Max Reinhardt's equally lavish and star-spangled *Midsummer Night's Dream* of the year before, moreover, Cukor's *Romeo and Juliet* remains one of the best Shakespeare films ever produced by a major Hollywood studio. It is not surprising, therefore, that the excerpts from *Othello* that Cukor staged in *A Double Life* (1947) would so distinguish that film.

Zaza (1938)

Romeo and Juliet, of course, presented little problem from the censorship standpoint when it was adapted to the screen, although some of the ribald exchanges of Romeo's roistering companions had to be trimmed from the text. But major surgery was required in order to bring the plot of *Zaza* into harmony with the tenets of the Motion Picture Code, which dictated that the May-December relationship of the young can-can dancer and a middle-aged married man had to be depicted as a passing romantic fancy that stopped short of adultery.

This severe undercutting of the original French play's frank treatment of marital infidelity robbed the movie of much of the conflict—and the credibility—of its source. To make matters worse, the production got off to a false start when the female lead had to be replaced, and Cukor had to begin all over again. Initially Paramount had hoped that the film would launch the American movie career of Italian diva Isa Miranda; but after shooting had commenced, the front office began to fear that Miranda's thick accent would be incomprehensible to American moviegoers, and she was replaced by Claudette Colbert. (Miranda later got her chance to do the role in Renato Castellani's Italian film version of the story, while she made her unmemorable American debut in Robert Forey's *Hotel Imperial* in 1939.)

Although Colbert was a sophisticated actress and was coached in her music-hall numbers by Cukor's friend the great musical-comedy star Fanny Brice, her depiction of Zaza does not radiate the kind of seductive allure that the part called for. She manages to make the role more her own, however, in the latter stages of the story when Zaza renounces her lover Dufresne (Herbert Marshall) after a chance meeting with his little girl which makes her realize that he has deceived her all along by denying that he is a family man.

Zaza subconsciously identifies with Dufresne's daughter because she herself grew up without a father, and she is determined not to deprive the girl of her father by taking Dufresne away from his family. In fact Zaza, emotionally speaking, is still something of a child at heart, as evidenced by the fact that her most prized possession is a doll which she has preserved from her own childhood days. Dufresne, then, is subconsciously a father figure as well as a lover for Zaza; and that makes it doubly hard for her to give him up when she sends him back to his family.

She bids him goodbye by singing him a farewell song from the stage during a performance while he listens from the back of the auditorium, aware that the song is meant especially for him. Then he resolutely turns his back on her and walks through the exit and out of her life for good. The last shot of the film shows Zaza accepting the applause of her devoted audience, as if, without being conscious of it, they are symbolically endorsing the sacrifice she has just made.

In spite of the careful alterations made in the screenplay in order to bring the story into harmony with the Code, the Code Commission made further censor cuts in the finished film. "According to the provisions of the Code at that time," Cukor explains, "a leading lady could not have an adulterous affair without suffering some kind of dreadful punishment, like breaking a leg or falling down a well." Since no such clear-cut physical punishment befell Zaza in the film, the Code Administration was at pains to make certain that no scene remained in the movie that hinted in any way whatever that Zaza and Dufresne had consummated their love. Hence the love scenes in the film were either truncated or deleted entirely.

Cukor rightly remarks that it is difficult to judge *Zaza* fairly, since the very heart of the story has been cut out of the movie. Nonetheless, even in the butchered version in which the movie exists, it is still in some ways a diverting picture that is worth seeing, if for no other reason than because it presents an affectionate toast to vaudeville as it was at the turn of the century which is highlighted by the delightful routines that feature the exuberant Bert Lahr.

Her Cardboard Lover (1942)

During this period Cukor made some other movies based on plays, which for various reasons are covered under other headings elsewhere in this book. But one film that deserves to be noted especially in a survey of his film versions of plays is *Her Cardboard Lover*, since, as already noted, it is the only work which Cukor directed on both stage and screen.

When asked by MGM to direct the movie adaptation of this bawdy French farce, Cukor agreed to do so. "But now I wish I hadn't," he says in retrospect. "The plot was already too dated to engage a wartime audience." In addition, Norma Shearer, like Laurette Taylor in the Cukor stage production before her, was a trifle too sedate to play the dizzy heroine of this cockeyed comedy.

The premise of the play is that a gay divorcée hires a gigolo to impersonate a fictitious fiancé in order to discourage her ex-husband from pressing her for a reconciliation. The play had been filmed twice before, once in the silent era as a vehicle for Marion Davies and once as a talkie entitled *The Passionate Plumber* starring Buster Keaton in the male lead. By the time the Cukor version came along, however, the Legion of Decency had been formed to rate the moral suitability of films for its Roman Catholic constituency; and the Legion frowned on divorce as a plot ingredient for a film. Because the Legion's ratings were followed by non-Catholics as well as by Catholics (in the absence of an industry rating system, which would not be formulated for another quarter of a century), the industry tended to do the Legion's bidding in order to avoid receiving an objectionable rating for a movie that could damage its chances at the box office. Hence in the present version of *Her Cardboard Lover* the ex-husband of the heroine, Consuela Croyden (Norma Shearer), becomes merely an ex-suitor.

It seems implausible that a young woman would go so far as to retain the services of a male companion to masquerade as her intended just to fend off an old boyfriend rather than a former husband, but then perhaps one should not expect a high degree of probability in a whimsical bit of fluff like *Her Cardboard Lover.*

In any case, the movie was soundly trounced by the reviewers, who said that Robert Taylor in the role of the hired man Terry Trindale had given a one-dimensional performance that merited his being called a cardboard lover. In fairness to Taylor, one must point out that not many actors could have brought off any better than he did the arch scene in which Terry emerges from Consuela's bedroom and greets her old beau Tony Barling (George Sanders) while wearing one of Consuela's nighties, in order to imply that Tony has caught him and Consuela *in flagrante delicto.* As Taylor plays the scene, Terry's behavior, which should appear outrageously funny, seems only a little coy and silly.

Still Cukor drew from both Shearer and Taylor better comic performances than they have been given credit for. Shearer is particularly good in the telephone scene in which she argues with Tony about the chances of their being reconciled, and Taylor's boyish charm is displayed to better advantage in this movie than in some of his other films of the period. And George Sanders, of course, is as suave as ever. But ultimately Cukor's clever direction could not rise above the mannered and self-conscious slapstick of the inane script, and the film's resounding failure hastened Norma Shearer's retirement from the screen. She never made another film.

Gaslight (1944)

On the other hand, *Gaslight* solidified the reputation of Ingrid Bergman as one of Hollywood's finest and most popular actresses, climaxed by her winning an Oscar for her performance. The play premiered in London in 1938, where it was an immediate hit, and was equally well received in the United States under the title of *Angel Street.* Thorold Dickinson directed an English film version of *Gaslight* in 1940 with Anton Walbrook and Diana Wynyard in the leads, and the film's success prompted MGM to do an American remake starring Ms. Bergman. Accordingly the studio bought the rights to the Dickinson film and withdrew it from circulation. The story that Metro destroyed all existing copies of the British film at that time is totally unfounded, however, since Dickinson's incarnation of the play has been screened both in Britain and America in recent years.

Nevertheless MGM's temporary suppression of the earlier film in order to clear the decks for its remake, released in 1944, enkindled a degree of indignant wrath among British film scholars and critics toward the Cukor version that has yet to abate fully. Thus Ivan Butler in *Cinema in Britain* scorns Cukor's American adaptation of the play as a travesty of Dickinson's English version; indeed, one can almost picture Butler hoisting the Union Jack as he inveighs against the American film of *Gaslight*.

A calmer, less partisan judgment of the relative merits of the two films has been expressed by Andrew Sarris, who readily concedes the virtues of Dickinson's tautly directed, compact motion picture. But he finds that Cukor's film, which is half an hour longer, possesses more richness of detail; a smoother, more substantial structure; and greater psychological depth.[6]

Cukor attributes the high quality of the screenplay of his American movie to the writing abilities of John Van Druten (whose play *Old Acquaintance* was the source of Cukor's film *Rich and Famous* in 1981) and of Walter Reisch (who had written scripts for Ernst Lubitsch). Reisch's forte was plot construction, while Van Druten's chief skill was composing dialogue. Together they worked over an earlier draft of the screenplay and came up with a superbly crafted shooting script.

In opening up the play for the screen, the writers wisely decided to dramatize certain crucial events which lead up to the point at which the action of the play gets under way. Hence the movie begins at the time of the murder of Alice Alquist, a renowned soprano, by Gregory Anton (Charles Boyer), who hopes to steal the precious jewels which she has hidden somewhere in her house. The film goes on to chronicle Anton's wooing and wedding of his victim's niece Paula (Ingrid Bergman), who has inherited the Alquist mansion, in order to continue frantically hunting for the missing diamonds.

When Paula and Gregory return from their apparently idyllic honeymoon on the Continent and move into the murder house, the movie then picks up on and develops the central action of the original play. Anton systematically sets about driving his doting wife insane, so that he can conveniently put her out of the way in an institution.

The title of the story derives from the gas jet in Paula's bedroom, which ominously dims whenever her husband turns on the gas lamp in the attic above in order to continue his ongoing search through Alice Alquist's belongings for the coveted gems. Since Anton sadistically encourages her to believe that she is only imagining this eerie phenomenon, the flickering gas flame in her room helps to increase Paula's fear that her reason is likewise beginning to waver.

In subtly tipping off the filmgoer fairly early on to what Anton is up to, Cukor has followed Hitchcock's principle of opting for prolonged suspense over momentary surprise in a thriller of this kind. Learning of Anton's duplicity only much later in the film, when Paula herself does, would have provided the moviegoer with a momentary shock of surprise. But by giving this vital information away to the viewer long before the heroine catches on, Cukor is able to build tension steadily in the filmgoer, who ruefully wonders throughout the balance of the movie if Paula will discover her husband's sordid scheme against her before it is too late.

At the climax of the movie, Paula at long last finds out that the husband to whom she has passionately devoted herself has never had any genuine feeling for her whatever, but rather has been enslaved all along to his obsessive addiction for diamonds, a passion which amounts to a perverse fetish that excludes the possibility of his really loving anything or anyone else.

In the gripping finale Paula revenges herself on her persecutor by pretending that she has in fact finally gone mad. Anton, who has been temporarily tied to a chair by a detective (Joseph Cotten), finds himself while in this helpless state of subjugation alone with the wife whom he has cruelly tormented. When he tries to charm her into freeing him from his bonds, she picks up a knife as if to comply—and pretends that she is going to cut his throat instead. She then watches with a quiet sense of exultation as the police finally take him away.

After seeing a preview of *Gaslight*, David O. Selznick, who had loaned Bergman and Cotten to MGM for the picture, suggested, among other things, that Cukor retake the final sequence in order to emphasize that her husband's imprisonment for his crimes will equivalently mean Paula's release from her bondage to him.[7] Cukor agreed; and because he also wanted to touch up some other aspects of this all-important scene as well, reshot the sequence, so that the picture now ends with Paula and the detective greeting the promising dawn together.

Selznick's memo also lauded the meticulous care with which the movie had been made, and was quite right to do so. For one thing,

visual metaphors abound in the film. The sinister shadow of the banister bars falling across Paula's face as she cowers on the winding staircase of her gloomy home implies the stifling, claustrophobic, jaillike atmosphere in which she lives. Moreover, the crafty, superficially charming husband who has captivated her is shown in the same shot standing on the landing above her, looking down on her both literally and figuratively from this position of dominance.

The key symbol of the fluttering gaslight is established during the credits while the voice of Alice Alquist is heard on the sound track wordlessly intoning "The Last Rose of Summer." Cukor implies in a variety of ways that the spirit of the dead soprano haunts the house where she was strangled, as Charles Higham has pointed out: a perfumed glove autographed for her by the great French composer Gounod reposes in a cabinet; Paula's off-screen voice describes the singer's death while the camera probes into the cavernous darkness of the fireplace near the spot where the corpse was found; and above the fireplace hangs the portrait of the deceased, wearing the very gown on which she enshrined among clusters of costume jewelry the priceless diamonds for which Anton lusts.[8] In the end Alice Alquist gets her own ironic revenge on Anton from the grave when he discovers the gems on the gown in the attic just before he is dragged off to prison, whereupon he loses them for good.

Cukor's sure hand with actors touched the performances of all of the players, including Angela Lansbury, who was still in her teens when she played the voluptuous serving girl who encourages Anton to take liberties with her. Ms. Lansbury, the daughter of English character actress Moyna MacGill, was already very much of a professional, despite her lack of experience, when Cukor tested her for the part. "Even though *Gaslight* was her first picture," Cukor remembers, "she had the ability to transform herself into the character that she was playing as soon as the cameras turned. I have always enjoyed coaching untried performers, and do not prefer to work exclusively with established actors, as has sometimes been said. In this instance I was very gratified that Angela received an Academy Award nomination for her very first time on screen."

Winged Victory (1944)

Cukor cast Angela Lansbury's mother, Moyna MacGill, as the winsome mother of an air cadet in *Winged Victory*. The script by Moss Hart was based on his own patriotic stage play about the trials of

Charles Boyer and Ingrid Bergman in Gaslight *(1944), for which she won an Academy Award.*

some young Air Force trainees. Prior to making this movie Cukor had
become familiar with life in the armed forces by doing a short hitch as
a private in the Signal Corps in 1942–43, during which he directed a
training film with the ponderous title of *Resistance and Ohm's Law*
(1943), about the theories of George Ohm, an eighteenth-century
physicist.

"I simply photographed an officer lecturing on this complicated
material," Cukor recalls. Neither Cukor nor the author of the
screenplay, playwright Arthur Laurents (*West Side Story*), had a clue
to what this complicated material was all about. "Arthur confessed to
me that he just took everything out of the training manual," Cukor
explains. "Yet this minor classic of ours won all sorts of commenda-
tions." Because he was more than forty when he was drafted, Cukor
was soon discharged as overage and returned to civilian life to draw
on his experiences in the armed forces for *Winged Victory*.

"*Winged Victory* was really a high class kind of training film" Cukor
comments, "a semi-documentary about a group of young Air Force
recruits and their trainers, all of whom were played by actors who
were actually members of the Army Air Force at the time." Many of
the young actors in the film had appeared in the Broadway production
of the play the previous year, and some of them would pursue screen
careers after the war. These included Pvt. Lon McAllister, Sgt.
Edmond O'Brien (who would appear in *A Double Life*), Cpl. Lee J.
Cobb, Cpl. Gary Merrill, and Cpl. Karl Malden—not to mention
Pvt. Martin Ritt, who would himself become an important film
director (*Hud*).

Speaking of fresh acting talent, it was in *Winged Victory*, not in
Adam's Rib (1949) as is often supposed, that Cukor first directed Judy
Holliday. "Darryl Zanuck, who produced *Winged Victory*, had seen
her in some little nightclub doing a comedy act with Betty Comden
and Adolph Green; and he asked me to test her," Cukor recalls. "I
thought that she was essentially a comedienne, but she played a
dramatic scene so movingly that I cast her as Ruth Miller, one of the
worried civilian wives." Holliday's unaffected warmth made her
stand out in the film, particularly in the scene in which Ruth consoles
Helen (Jeanne Crain) on the night that their husbands take off for
overseas.

Although *Winged Victory* was a fairly routine war film, Cukor
brought to it all of his cinematic creativity in order to enliven the
material in whatever way he could. He sums up the transition from
civilian life to army life for the new recruits by cutting from a close-up

of one young man's two-toned saddle shoes and argyles to a shot of his brand-new army boots and leggings. Cukor epitomizes the intensive training course which the awkward new cadets must undergo in a montage sequence in which he photographs them at times from tilted camera angles to indicate how they are caught off balance by being plunged so swiftly into the rituals of army life and discipline. He accompanies these shots on the sound track by a chorus of instructors' voices barking commands and admonitions which cumulatively overwhelm the young trainees.

For all of the documentary authenticity with which Cukor flavors the film, however, the air cadets as drawn in Hart's idealistic screenplay seem a shade too clean cut and boisterously exuberant to represent young men going off to fight in a very grim war. Hence there is some truth in James Agee's capsule review of this morale-boosting film in the *Nation*. "*Winged Victory* has some briskly interesting and well-assembled material about the training and testing and rejecting phases of Air Force life," he wrote; "but I don't enjoy having anyone try to persuade me, so cheerfully and energetically, that the Air Force personnel is without exception composed of boy scouts old enough to shave."[9]

A Double Life (1947)

After the war Cukor made a film called *A Double Life*, from an original screenplay by the husband-wife writing team of Garson Kanin and Ruth Gordon, who between them would be responsible for six more film scripts for Cukor. Admittedly *A Double Life* was not adapted from a stage play, but I include it in this chapter because the story is constructed around a production of *Othello* and because the film deals so explicitly with Cukor's ongoing theme, exemplified throughout this chapter, about the need for one to distinguish between illusion and reality in life.

As already mentioned, this theme applies in a special way to show-business types who, like the hero of *A Double Life*, are apt to become lost in the world of illusion which they create for others. Yet Cukor implies in this movie, as in his other films, that in one sense all of us lead a double life that moves between illusion and reality as we seek to sort out fantasy from fact in an effort to deal realistically with our problems.

In *A Double Life* Ronald Colman portrays Anthony John, an actor who becomes so identified with his stage roles that he develops a

murderous streak of jealousy while playing Othello during a long
Broadway run. With increasing difficulty he tries to divorce himself
from the role when he is offstage, until he ultimately goes insane and
strangles a prostitute.

The dark, brooding atmosphere of the film, coupled with the
equally cynical, somber vision of life reflected in this tale of obsession, despair, and death, marks the movie as an example of *film noir*.
This trend in American cinema, which also includes other Cukor
films like *Keeper of the Flame* (1943) and *A Life of Her Own* (1950),
was flourishing when *A Double Life* was made; and the pessimistic
view of life exhibited in such movies, itself an outgrowth of the
disillusionment spawned by World War II and the period of uncer-
tainty that was its aftermath, is clearly in evidence in *A Double Life*.
In keeping with the conventions of *film noir*, this motion picture is
characterized by an air of grim, unvarnished realism, typified by the
stark, newsreellike quality of the location scenes shot around New
York City, so many of which ominously take place under cover of
darkness.

In the movie's strongest scene Anthony John is spending the
evening with his mistress Pat Kroll (Shelley Winters), a full-time
waitress at a café appropriately called the Venezia and a part-time
prostitute. When John becomes obsessed with the idea that she is still
seeing other men, Othello's obsessional jealousy begins to seep into
the actor's consciousness and to possess him completely. As Pat asks
him to switch off the light, she unwittingly brings to his mind a snatch
of dialogue from the murder scene of *Othello*, which was shown in
performance earlier in the film. John, now transported into this scene
of the play, hears the voice of Desdemona (Signe Hasso) request him
to extinguish the lamp in her bedroom before she drifts off to sleep. In
his role as Othello, John quenches instead the life within Pat Kroll,
thinking all the while that it is Desdemona that he is sending off to
sleep forever.

While John throttles the life out of this wretched creature, an
elevated train thunders by the window of Pat's squalid flat; and its
nerve-jangling clamor is a fit accompaniment for the ugly violence
taking place inside. Indeed, this unsettling noise is more effective
than any background music could have been at this point.

The creative use of sound in this sequence is matched by equally
creative camera work. As Pat falls backward on the bed in death, the
camera catches in close-up her hand pulling across the foot of the bed
the curtain that separates her bedroom from the rest of her scruffy

little flat. Her action recalls the way in which Desdemona in a similar fashion reaches up from her bed and closes the drapery of her sumptuous fourposter as she breathes her last. These complementary images accentuate still more the close parallel between Pat's murder in real life and that of Desdemona in the play.

The movie ends with an equally striking bit of visual imagery. After the police have discovered with the help of John's press agent (Edmond O'Brien) that the actor is the killer they are after, they go to the theater and wait for him backstage while he finishes what is to be his last performance. Once more merging illusion with reality, John plays Othello's suicide scene with a real dagger, and ends his own life as he ends the play. The film's final, unforgettable image is that of the curtains parting to allow the star to take his bows—while the spotlight reveals only an empty stage. The slow dimming of the spotlight beam into darkness thus signals the fading away of a once-great star in the theatrical firmament.

For old time's sake Cukor used the old Empire Theater in New York City to shoot all of the scenes in the film that take place on stage, since the Empire is where he worked for Gilbert Miller in the 1920s. While filming portions of a performance of *Othello* on the Empire's stage, Cukor had cinematographer Milton Krasner shoot directly into the banks of spotlights and footlights on the stage, thereby giving the filmgoer some sense of what a theatrical performance is like from the point of view of the actors. This approach is particularly effective when John commits suicide, since viewing the actor's suicide from the vantage point of the other actors on stage with him at the time serves to involve the viewer in the action much more deeply than if the scene had been photographed from the more distant point of view of the audience in the theater.

"When I discussed the suicide scene with Ronnie Colman," Cukor remembers, "I said that a light should come into John's eyes just before he expires, as if he was experiencing a last surge of life at the moment of death. When I looked at the rushes the next day there it was! He really knew how to act for the camera." The Motion Picture Academy thought so, too, and conferred an Oscar on Colman for his performance in *A Double Life*.

Shelley Winters was still relatively new to pictures when she played opposite Colman in the film; but he was very kind to her, even though she proved sassy and temperamental at times. Asked about the story that Ms. Winters's behavior so exasperated the director at one point that he gave her a whack to shut her up, Cukor responds

with a twinkle, "If I did I am sure she deserved it. She was inexperienced, pushy, and brash; and I had to tell her to pipe down and listen to direction many times."

Cukor's work with Angela Lansbury on *Gaslight,* however, indicates his natural inclination to be helpful to and supportive of neophyte actors if they are willing to cooperate with him. As Ms. Lansbury remarked at the Lincoln Center tribute to Cukor in 1978, she was very young and inexperienced when she auditioned for Cukor; "and I didn't know my ass from a hole in the ground. He introduced me to style."[10]

The Model and the Marriage Broker (1951)

The Model and the Marriage Broker is a minor film in the Cukor canon, a movie he made to fulfill a contractual obligation at Fox. Though it is not based on a stage play, I am rounding off this chapter by considering it briefly here because, like *A Double Life,* it does bring into relief Cukor's predilection for depicting the collision of fact and fantasy in people's lives. In this instance this theme is exemplified in a group of lonely hearts who seek the services of a professional match maker to find them the mate of their dreams, but often wind up settling for someone who falls short of the ideal partner they had hoped for. As the marriage broker observes at one point, "You can get used to being poor or even blind; but not to being lonely."

Cukor became involved in this project as something of an afterthought. "Metro lent me to Fox to direct a picture which fell through when the screenplay didn't pan out," says Cukor; "and so I agreed to stay on at Fox and make *The Model and the Marriage Broker,* although ordinarily I would have turned down a modest little picture like this, since by that time I had become a little too 'grand' to direct a film that wasn't a class A production." Still he enjoyed working with Milton Krasner, who had photographed *A Double Life,* "and with the adorable Thelma Ritter," who played the kind of loveable middleaged eccentrics to which Judy Holliday would have graduated had she lived longer.

In the movie Ms. Ritter plays Mae Swazey, the gabby, feisty match maker of the title. Her clientele consists mostly of a mixed bag of misfits whose behavior is at once funny and touching. One of her customers, George Wixted (Zero Mostel), tries to ingratiate himself with a young lady whom he is fitting for eye-glasses by assuring her that she is one of the few women whose appearance is actually

Signe Hasso and Ronald Colman in a scene from Othello *in* A Double Life. *Colman won an Oscar as an actor "consumed by the fires of his own greatness," as the ads put it.*

enhanced by wearing spectacles; and that, he points out, is the highest compliment a man in his profession can bestow on a lady.

When one of Mae's charges (played by Scott Brady, a bargain basement version of Aldo Ray) decides at the last moment to leave his bride at the altar because he cannot bear to be yoked to her ferocious, saber-toothed mother as well, the irrepressible Mae offers this homespun consolation to the erstwhile groom: "I bet old satchel hips will be eating the chicken à la king [prepared for the canceled reception] for the next six weeks." The young man eventually marries the model of the title, with the help of Mae's ministrations.

The warmth and good humor with which Cukor treats the not-so-swinging singles in the film illustrates that, although the director may question the unrealistic dreams the characters in his films sometimes nourish, he never withholds his compassion—or that of his audience—from these brokenhearted dreamers when their illusions are inevitably shattered.

The primary purpose of the present chapter has been to explore several of the Cukor films that have been based on stage plays or deal with theatrical illusions of life, in order to demonstrate how he seeks to transfer theatrical works to the screen with freshness and imagination. Perhaps there is no better way to crystallize the relationship of film and theater as reflected in Cukor's movie versions of plays than in citing Pauline Kael's valentine to filmed theater: "Some of the most enjoyable movies ever made—such as George Cukor's *Dinner at Eight*—are well-made adaptations of plays," she writes. "Filmed plays are often denigrated, somewhat dishonestly, by people who learn a little about what is said to be proper to the film medium and forget about the pleasure they've been getting from filmed plays all their lives."[11]

No small measure of that pleasure has been provided by the screen adaptations of plays directed by George Cukor.

3

The Dynamic Duo:
Tracy and Hepburn

GEORGE CUKOR'S PROFESSIONAL ALLIANCE with Katharine Hepburn and Spencer Tracy proved to be one of the most durable cinematic associations between a director and a pair of actors in the history of motion pictures. Cukor directed Tracy and Hepburn separately and as a team in a total of twelve films. Although all three of these individuals possessed decidedly independent temperaments, they learned early on to work well together; and the chemistry of their mutual relationship produced some excellent films.

A Bill of Divorcement (1932)

Katharine Hepburn's first appearance in a Cukor movie was in *A Bill of Divorcement*, which also happened to be the first movie that she ever made. In this adaptation of Clemence Dane's British play she took the part of Sydney Fairchild, a young woman who gives up her plans for marriage to take care of her mentally disturbed father, Hilary (John Barrymore), and also to avoid the possibility of perpetuating the insanity that runs in the family in the children she might have had.

Cukor recalls buttonholing Adela Rogers St. Johns, one of the authors of Cukor's *What Price Hollywood?* (1932), when he met her on the RKO lot one hot afternoon right after he had seen Ms. Hepburn's screen test for *Bill of Divorcement*. "Nobody wants her but me; so come and help me fight for her," he exclaimed. "She looks like a boa constrictor on a fast, but she's great!"

Hollywood technicians had not yet learned how to photograph Ms. Hepburn's angular looks to best advantage or to record her clipped, metallic New England accent properly; so the screen test was not

An immortal trio: Spencer Tracy, Katharine Hepburn, and George Cukor on location for Pat and Mike *(1952).*

very successful. On the other hand, she had shrewdly chosen to do a scene for her test from a play that she was totally familiar with, Philip Barry's *Holiday,* in which she had understudied the lead for six months in New York in 1929, instead of picking a scene from *A Bill of Divorcement* as the other actresses trying out for the part had done. Cukor was particularly impressed by the touch of class that Ms. Hepburn displayed in the course of the test in the way in which she swept down and picked up a glass of wine from the floor, a gesture which reflected that she was very much in command of herself and of the situation.

Despite the front office's misgivings about Cukor's wish to choose newcomer Hepburn over such proved talents as Norma Shearer and Irene Dunne to play opposite John Barrymore in *Bill of Divorcement,* Cukor was convinced of Ms. Hepburn's potential as a screen actress and stuck to his guns. David O. Selznick, head of production at RKO, finally supported Cukor's choice for the role of Sydney because he believed that "the story would be more moving and believeable if it was played by a girl that hadn't previously been identified with other parts."[1]

Once chosen for the part, Ms. Hepburn radiated a sense of self-possession around the studio that was quite uncommon in a new arrival. When she imperiously rejected some of the costume designs for the role of Sydney, Cukor took one look at the casually mismatched shirt and slacks she was wearing and retorted, "How can you consider yourself an authority on clothes when your own wardrobe is the damndest thing I've ever seen!" With that, he took her up to the studio hairdresser and had her hair cut, he continues; "and there for the first time was the real Katharine Hepburn."

John Barrymore gave a low-key performance in the film which, like his portrayal of Larry Renault in *Dinner at Eight* the following year, was completely devoid of the theatrical mannerisms and histrionics that sometimes marred his screen work for other directors. Barrymore's first entrance in the film occurs when Hilary returns to the Fairchild manor house for the first time since he had been committed to a mental institution many years before when Sydney was still an infant. As Hilary silently explores the drawing room of the house that was once his home, his actions are tentative, his gaze remote; all of the unfamiliar objects he sees around him force him to realize that life has gone on without him.

Meanwhile Sydney sits on the staircase nearby, furtively watching her father through the banister bars. Then she summons the courage to move from behind the barrier that separates her from the father whom she has never met, and introduce herself to him with infinite love and compassion. When Barrymore saw the tears streaming down Ms. Hepburn's cheeks at the end of this scene, he winked at Cukor and said, "She's okay."

Throughout filming, Barrymore always favored the young actress in every scene that they played together, by consistently directing attention away from himself to her whenever he could. Years later Ms. Hepburn sought to repay the kindness Barrymore had shown her during the shooting of *Bill of Divorcement* by seeking without success to find Barrymore work in pictures at a time when his career was foundering.

In the last scene of the film Sydney is once more alone with her father. Kit, Sydney's ex-fiancé, whom she has renounced in order to stay with her father, can be heard outside the house whistling the melody that had been their secret lovers' signal, in a last desperate effort to make her change her mind. Sydney resolutely closes the window curtains to insulate herself from the sound, and sits down next to Hilary at the piano to play a duet with him. The swelling chords drown out Kit's tune still more, and also testify to the complete harmony that has developed between father and daughter, as the film draws to a close.

Given the critical and commercial success of *A Bill of Divorcement*, RKO decided to remake the film in 1940 with Maureen O'Hara and Adolphe Menjou in the leads. Reviews of the latter film, directed by John Farrow and retitled *Never to Love*, generally favored Cukor's film as a more distinguished treatment of the same material and singled out Ms. O'Hara's performance as no match for that given by Ms. Hepburn in the earlier version.

A Bill of Divorcement, in fact, unequivocally established Katharine Hepburn as the star Cukor knew she could be—despite the fact that her first name was misspelled as Katherine in the cast list of the movie's credits. One critic pinpointed her uniqueness by describing her as a dynamic, well-trained screen actress in a profession overrun at the time with characterless, synthetic blondes. Concerning his part in shaping her screen career, Cukor once wrote to me in a facetious vein that movies like *Bill of Divorcement* and *Little Women* offer "proof positive that I was her Svengali."[2] But there is more than a little truth in this statement, as Ms. Hepburn would be the first to admit; for she continued to respond to his knowledgeable and sympathetic guidance as they made more pictures together.

Little Women (1933)

Cukor's second picture with Katharine Hepburn, *Little Women*, was part of the Hollywood trend of the period to make films of classic literary works—also exemplified in Cukor's *David Copperfield* (1935) and *Romeo and Juliet* (1936)—in order to attract a large family audience. While Cukor and Selznick were still working together at RKO, Selznick decided to make a sound version of *Little Women*, which had first been filmed in 1919. Although Cukor and Selznick prepared the film for production, they left RKO for Metro before shooting could be started, and made *Dinner at Eight* (1933). But Cukor still owed RKO a picture, and so he fulfilled his contractual obligation to that studio by returning to direct *Little Women* with Katharine Hepburn as Jo March, as originally planned.

The Louisa May Alcott novel tells the story of the four March girls living with their mother in Concord, Massachusetts, while their father is away fighting in the Civil War and they are trying to be the responsible "little women" he expects them to be in his absence. While Selznick was still involved with the project at RKO, he wisely dissuaded RKO executives from attempting to "modernize" the story by moving the time in which it is set up to the present day, since *Little Women* is so thoroughly saturated with the austere atmosphere of Civil War New England.

Accordingly, the studio assigned New York artist Hobe Erwin to create the period sets. Erwin did a flawless job, even going so far as to model the March home after Louisa May Alcott's own house. The snow-capped roof of the March home in the winter scenes early in the film is an effective symbol of the chill of civil war that hangs over the land and genuinely brings the period to life.

Cukor's spare, immaculate direction keeps the story from turning to sugar, no easy task when a film has as many sad scenes as this one does. The most tearful episode is the death from scarlet fever of Jo's invalid sister Beth (Jean Parker), an incident lifted from *Good Wives*, a sequel to *Little Women*. On the day that Beth's death scene was shot, the sound men at the studio were on strike, and the amateur sound crew that was temporarily brought in to keep the picture on schedule kept ruining take after take by not recording the dialogue properly. Finally, after at least sixteen takes, the scene was in the can. "I had cried so many times by then," Ms. Hepburn recalls, "that I just threw up!"[3]

Katharine Hepburn with John Barrymore in her first film, A Bill of Divorcement *(1932).*

After Tallulah Bankhead had seen a rough cut of some footage from the film, she was so overwhelmed by Ms. Hepburn's depiction of the headstrong yet vulnerable Jo that she fell on her knees before the young actress and sobbed uncontrollably. Cukor, who was standing nearby, commented, "Tallulah, you are weeping for your own lost innocence." Expanding on this remark, Cukor adds that the fundamental appeal of *Little Women* is not just to children but to adults, whom it allows to relive nostalgically the period of their own youth.

Cukor has managed to capture the youthful spirit of the novel on film so successfully, writes Gary Carey, that the movie's most compelling images remain in the memory long after one has seen the picture. There is the eye-filling party scene, all waltzing couples, ruffles, and frills, which creates "one of the loveliest moments of Americana in all of film"; and Jo sitting on the grass "with brilliant diffused sunlight around her," gently but firmly refusing a young admirer's proposal of marriage because she is determined to make her way in the world as a writer before she weds. *Little Women,* Carey concludes, is Cukor's most beautifully lit and imaginatively photographed film up to that time; "but, as is typical of Cukor, nothing calls attention to itself."[4]

Indeed, Cukor's skillfully composed shots evoke nineteenth-century America so genuinely that one might almost say that if the technical equipment to make a movie had been available in the 1860s, the films made at that time would look exactly like Cukor's *Little Women*! Critics applauded the movie as an antidote to the febrile gangster films and backstage musicals of the period, and thus as a welcome reminder that authentic emotions could still be stirred by an unpatronizing screen version of a classic novel as well as by machine guns and precision dancers. Moreover, the movie went on to win an Academy Award for Sarah Mason and Victor Heerman's superb screenplay and a best actress award for Katharine Hepburn at the 1934 Cannes Film Festival.

Giving his personal reflections on movie making in a 1938 essay, Cukor revealed the method he had developed in working with a challenging actress like Katharine Hepburn. "She is a human dynamo," he wrote; and because of the vigor and intensity of her approach to film acting, she could be, without realizing it, rather stubborn in insisting on playing a scene her way. Consequently, while directing her in *Little Women,* he developed an effective technique in collaborating with her. "I confess freely that I used many weapons in dealing with her; simulated rage, ridicule, and good-humored cajolery." His approach worked, he confided, because "she has a great sense of humor, and is quite capable of directing it toward herself."[5]

The 1933 *Little Women* is a personal favorite of both Cukor and Hepburn; hence, Cukor refused Selznick's plea to take over from Mervyn LeRoy the direction of the 1949 remake of *Little Women.* "David asked me to discuss the matter with Daniel O'Shea, his Irish Machiavellian aide," says Cukor. "And so I found myself standing in front of the Selznick studios at 9 o'clock one Sunday morning. Suddenly an inconspicuous door that I never knew existed before opened in the studio wall, and I was spirited into a projection room to look at some of the footage that the other director had already shot, featuring David's wife Jennifer Jones as Jo."

Afterward Cukor told O'Shea that Katharine Hepburn came from a large New England family and had so identified with the novel's spirit of familial feeling "that she had cast a magic spell over the entire production; and without her that magic simply wouldn't be there. Besides, I did the picture once as well as I knew how; and there is no point in my redoing it."

Mervyn LeRoy stayed on as director, but Selznick subsequently sold the production package to MGM, which went ahead filming the remake with June Allyson as Jo. "Our film had a purity that was based on a respect for the period setting," says Cukor; whereas the slick style of the Metro version "looked more like present-day Beverly Hills than nineteenth century Concord, Massachusetts."

Once again, as with *Bill of Divorcement,* a Cukor film had been remade in a version that in no way superceded his original treatment of the same material. And the same can be said about the soppy 1978 TV adaptation of *Little Women,* which likewise failed to obscure the brilliance of the 1933 *Little Women.*

Sylvia Scarlett (1936)

Cukor returned to RKO for the last time to direct Katharine Hepburn in *Sylvia Scarlett* (1936), the first of three Cukor films in which she would costar with Cary Grant. But, unlike *Little Women, Sylvia Scarlett* was a resounding flop. Cukor comments that it had something gallant and foolhardy about it: "It has some interesting things in it which an audience seems to enjoy today, but that was not the case when it was originally released. We all had a good time making it, but somehow I never got the film to work. Perhaps the storyline became too complicated as it unfolded."

The movie is based on the first volume of Compton MacKenzie's *Sylvia Scarlett* trilogy and opens with this printed preface: "To the adventurer, to all who stray from the beaten track, life is an extravagance in which laughter and luck and love come in odd ways; but they are nonetheless sweet for that." This preface is a toast to those who seek to fulfill their romantic illusions in life; for, as Allen Estrin has noted, Cukor recognizes that, although we must always be ready to face reality, "we all need an occasional respite from it."[6] The first part of the film is very much in harmony with these sentiments.

At the beginning we follow the adventures of Sylvia (Katharine Hepburn), her father (Edmund Gwenn), and their cockney companion in skulduggery, Jimmy Monkley (Cary Grant), as they swindle and con their way around England. Since Sylvia's father already had a police record in France before coming to England, Sylvia dresses as a boy and calls herself "Sylvester Scarlett" so that they will escape detection. But her disguise also betokens the unreal existence that she is living with the other two. The trio becomes further enmeshed in illusion when they become strolling players after they tire of a life of petty crime.

A crisis arises, however, when Sylvia begins to fall in love, first with Jimmy and then with Michael Fane, an artist (Brian Aherne). In effect, she has to choose between living in the real world with Michael or continuing to inhabit a world of fantasy with Jimmy. Sylvia finally faces reality, drops her disguise, and admits her feelings for Michael. But in doing so she has turned her back, however reluctantly, on Jimmy and the madcap existence that he represents. Cukor seems to harbor some degree of affection for the world of romantic illusion, for there is usually a hint of regret in his films when reality inevitably impinges itself on the world of one of his dreamers, a world in which "laughter and luck and love come in odd ways; but they are nonetheless sweet for that."

Cukor and his collaborators thought that they had made a bittersweet romantic comedy, and were quite taken aback when the film was considered by some to be a daring examination of Sylvia's sexual ambiguity. That Sylvia feels more at home wearing trousers rather than a skirt for a substantial portion of the film, however, was instead intended to suggest that she fundamentally remains an adolescent tomboy until she at last falls in love with Michael and emerges as the attractive young woman she was always destined to be.

The scenes in which Sylvia gets into embarrassing scrapes because of her male masquerade, furthermore, were designed to be funny and not slyly perverse in intent, as when a seasick Sylvia cannot decide whether to head for the ship's men's room or its ladies' room, and finally winds up heaving over the rail. Later on Michael wonders for a time why he finds Sylvester Scarlett so fetching, until he discovers much to his relief that Sylvester is really Sylvia. Similar situations as the last one just described develop in the Shakespeare comedies in which the heroine temporarily disguises herself as a young man, such as *As You Like It* and *Twelfth Night* (both of which, interestingly enough, Ms. Hepburn later appeared in on the stage), and are quite in keeping with the conventions of classical theater. But the mass movie audience apparently found such episodes in the film more disturbing than humorous, despite the fact that just before the film's release a scene was added at the very beginning of the picture in order to establish Sylvia's essential femininity from the outset. In it Sylvia is shown dressed very much as a girl prior to her shearing off her long tresses and donning masculine attire.

But no amount of tampering with the film could induce moviegoers to take *Sylvia Scarlett* to their hearts when it was originally released. Cukor already feared that the jig was up when he attended a sneak preview of the picture. "It was a ghastly preview, held in a theater in a town on the California coast," he remembers. "The audience began walking out half way through the picture, and those that stayed kept laughing in all the wrong places." For her part, Katharine Hepburn recalls that when she retreated to the ladies' room during the preview, she found a woman prostrate on a sofa recovering from a dead faint. With all of the good humor which she could muster under the circumstances, Ms. Hepburn inquired sympathetically, "Did our picture finish you off?" She got no reply.

To make amends for the film's fiasco, Cukor and Hepburn generously offered to do another picture without charge for the movie's desolate producer, Pandro Berman, if he were willing to scrap *Sylvia Scarlett*. Berman ruefully responded that the studio could not afford to shelve the picture, and that he would never work with either of them again. (As a matter of fact, Cukor later directed *Bhowani Junction* [1956] and *Justine* [1969] for Berman, and Ms. Hepburn's next four films after *Sylvia* were all produced by him.)

Just about the only individual who came off with good notices for the film was Cary Grant. Hitherto Grant had played conventional romantic screen heroes. By casting him as a very unconventional rogue, Cukor enabled Grant to expand his acting range by trying his hand at a character role. "It was the first film in which Cary felt at home in front of a camera," Cukor remarks. "He gave a wonderful performance, but that didn't save the picture at the time." In actuality, the film's sophisticated style of black comedy was really ahead of

Katharine Hepburn in two gamine roles: (top) masquerading as a male in Sylvia
Scarlett *(with a startled Brian Aherne); (bottom) with Cary Grant in* Holiday *(1938),
one of two Philip Barry plays they filmed with Cukor.*

its time, and *Sylvia Scarlett* has over the years developed a cult following.

Holiday (1938)

Undaunted by the largely negative reception of *Sylvia Scarlett*, Cukor, Hepburn, and Grant regrouped their forces to make the screen versions of two Philip Barry plays, the first of which was *Holiday*, which had been filmed in 1930 as a primitive talkie with Ann Harding in the lead. As mentioned earlier, Ms. Hepburn had understudied the same role on Broadway, and had done a scene from *Holiday* for her screen test in 1932. So it was no surprise that Cukor agreed with her that she should play the key part of Linda Seton in the film of *Holiday*, which Cukor was remaking at Columbia.

The new screenplay was principally the work of Donald Ogden Stewart, one of Cukor's favorite screen writers, who had in fact created the role of the hero's sidekick Nick Potter in the original Broadway production. In addition, Stewart, whose association with the playwright dated back to their college days at Yale, had a real feel for Barry's work, as his screenplay clearly attests.

The story focuses on Linda Seton (Katharine Hepburn), a wealthy young lady bored and frustrated by the insulated life of luxury which she leads with her stuffy family in the cold, marble mausoleum which they inhabit on Fifth Avenue. Hence she often takes refuge in the cozy warmth of the nursery room where she grew up in order to get away from them all. Linda's behavior represents an obvious retreat from reality into a never-never land where she surrounds herself with all sorts of souvenirs of her childhood, including a Punch and Judy puppet theater and some cuddly toy animals, and where she is free to contemplate her youthful fantasies and longings.

Into this dream world bursts Johnny Case (Cary Grant), her sister Julia's effervescent fiancé, who possesses all the spunk and drive which Linda lacks. The exuberant Johnny manages to shake her out of her lethargic existence, however, to the point where she is moved to endorse his refusal to join the family firm, which he resentfully senses is the price he is expected to pay for acceptance into the Seton clan. Johnny accordingly breaks his engagement to Julia and elopes with Linda. Her resolve to go off with Johnny is strengthened by her awareness that her brother Ned (Lew Ayres) has ruined his life by constantly knuckling under to the family's imperious demands on him, and he has thus retreated into alcoholism as his particular form of escape.

The heart of both the play and the film is the extended scene played out in Linda's childhood playroom on the night of the New Year's Eve party at which Johnny's foredoomed engagement to Julia is to be announced.

To escape the boring stuffed shirts attending the formal function, Johnny and Linda stage an impromptu counterparty in the nursery for a few of their intimates, including Nick Potter (Edward Everett Horton, repeating the role of Johnny's old buddy which he played in the 1930 film). Cukor keeps his camera on the go, moving from one character to another as it roves about the room, in order to catch every significant gesture and remark, so that the viewer hardly notices that the action rarely strays from this single central setting throughout the sequence. As Johnny and Linda dance to the sprightly tune of her music box, it is clear that they are much more in harmony with each other than they are with the haughty guests solemnly waltzing at the official gala elsewhere in the house. The scene ends prophetically with the two of them greeting the new year together. Life with the unpredictable Johnny may not always prove to be a holiday, but Linda is willing to take her chances.

Ms. Hepburn gave a grand performance in *Holiday*, and *Time* pointed out that the film emphatically gave the lie to the recent proclamation of the Independent Theater Owners of America (made, no doubt, with films like *Sylvia Scarlett* in mind) that she was "box office poison." Besides, nearly everyone agreed that *Holiday* was a well-executed movie, and Gary Carey is correct in contending that this is because it is just the kind of motion picture that Cukor does best. "There is a strong human situation at its center and strong characters that can be developed, and are worth the camera's time spent lingering over them," he notes. "There is not a single misplaced camera set-up or ill-judged cut in the film."[7]

The Philadelphia Story (1940)

The Philadelphia Story was the third Cukor film in which Katharine Hepburn costarred with Cary Grant. The original play on which the movie was based had already begun to take shape shortly after the filming of *Holiday* had been completed. Philip Barry was so entranced with Ms. Hepburn's performance in *Holiday* that he showed her the outline of this projected stage work even before he had written the first draft. Ms. Hepburn in turn was so captivated by the central role of Tracy Lord that she had the foresight to purchase the screen rights of *The Philadelphia Story* in order to insure that she could play the same part when the play was subsequently filmed.

After the play's successful launching on Broadway, she sold MGM a package which included herself as star, Cukor as director, and Donald Ogden Stewart as screen writer, along with no less than two established male stars, Cary Grant and James Stewart, to add luster to the proceedings and to enhance the film's box-office potential. To produce this already prestigious production, Metro chose Joseph L. Mankiewicz, who would himself one day be a major director (*All About Eve*).

The picture was shot in the summer of 1940, between the time that Hepburn closed in the New York production of the play and she took it on the road the following autumn. Consequently Cukor had to make the movie version on a tight eight-week schedule. He managed to complete principal photography on time, however, with virtually no retakes; but there is no hint of haste visible in the finished product.

Because Ms. Hepburn was recreating on film a part she had already played more than four hundred times on the stage, Cukor was at pains throughout shooting to ward off the possibility of her performance going slightly stale. He accomplished this by "discombobulating" the actress at times. He would, for example, direct her not to cry during a scene in which she had wept on the stage, and in this way kept her performance fresh and spontaneous. Little wonder that Ms. Hepburn won the New York Critics Award for her portrayal of Tracy Lord, since it represents her definitive portrait of a domineering, supersophisticated young socialite, who nevertheless retains a disarming vulnerability.

In the opening scene, a wordless prologue not in the play, Tracy arrogantly evicts her husband, Dexter Haven (Cary Grant), from the Lord mansion after a domestic quarrel, snapping one of his golf clubs over her knee for good measure. Dexter retaliates by flattening Tracy with a push in the face. With devilish ingenuity Dexter later gets even with Tracy for rejecting him in favor of George Kittredge, an insipid social climber, by inviting himself to the wedding and bringing along with him Mike Connor (James Stewart) and Liz Imbrie (Ruth Hussey), a reporter and a photographer for a tacky gossip magazine called *Spy,* just to embarrass his former spouse.

James Stewart won an Oscar for his easygoing performance as the young man who seeks to convince Tracy that, despite her frosty facade, she is lit from within by fires that are banked deep down inside her. He is thus able to melt Tracy's icy exterior and to reveal the warm human being underneath. Then he gallantly turns her over to her rollicking ex-husband, Dexter, whom she at last is prepared to accept as he really is, now that she has abandoned her unrealistic search for the ideal husband and sent Kittredge packing.

Donald Stewart also received an Academy Award for coming up with a literate screenplay that was appropriately faithful to the spirit of the Barry original. Like *Holiday*, the chief virtue of *The Philadelphia Story* is its witty, brittle dialogue. Therefore, as the camera focuses on the cross-section of characters assembled for the wedding festivities and cuts from one knot of guests to another, Cukor wisely gives special emphasis to their scintillating repartee just as he had done in the earlier film.

On the other hand, the director does not neglect the visual component of the movie for the sake of the verbal, as illustrated by the film's first scene, mentioned above, which niftily distills into a single sequence the flavor of Tracy and Dexter's stormy married life without the need of a single line of dialogue. The childish, spiteful behavior of the two principals speaks for itself; and the hilarious episode was later included in MGM's anthology film *That's Entertainment II* (1976) as a first-class example of visual comedy.

The movie also ends with a telling visual image. As Dexter and Tracy make their second trip to the altar together, someone snaps a picture of them which freezes into a photograph reproduced in the pages of *Spy* magazine. Cukor's inventive use of the freeze frame to stop the characters in mid-action at film's end suggests that their lives will go on after the film is over, and antedates by a couple of decades the overuse of this device by other directors in recent years to make the same point.

Cukor's accomplishment in making *The Philadelphia Story* as delightful a farce on screen as it was in the theater stands out in relief all the more when one compares it to the musical remake of his film done by Charles Walters in 1956 under the title of *High Society*. The later movie, which boasted Bing Crosby, Grace Kelly, and Frank Sinatra in the roles played in Cukor's film by Cary Grant, Katharine Hepburn, and James Stewart, plodded along listlessly because Walters simply lacked Cukor's flair for imparting a brisk pace and a light touch to sophisticated comedy of this kind. Moreover, the principal performers in *High Society* were not nearly as gifted as their counterparts in the earlier picture with a talent for playing high comedy.

To make matters worse, a great deal of the original screenplay's delightful dialogue was shorn away to make room in the musical remake for a mediocre Cole Porter score, written in the great composer's twilight years. In short, one can only wonder why anyone felt the need to make a musical out of *The Philadelphia Story,* when Cukor in effect had already "set it to music" with the finely tuned ensemble acting of his definitive screen version of the play.

Keeper of the Flame (1943)

After directing Katharine Hepburn in a trio of films in which she costarred with Cary Grant, Cukor made another three films with her in the next few years at Metro in which she was paired with Spencer Tracy, whom he also directed in two other films as well during the same period. Although Cukor's first opportunity to direct the team came with *Keeper of the Flame,* Ms. Hepburn had initially hoped that Cukor could have directed her first film with Tracy, *Women of the Year* (1942); but the director was still occupied at the time with filming Garbo's last picture, *Two-Faced Woman* (1941).

Although Cukor and Tracy had both been at Metro for some time, the two men had hardly met until Ms. Hepburn brought them together socially; and even then there was still a considerable amount of speculation in the film colony about whether or not the actor and the director could work well together. Cukor was known to be a perfectionist who did not mind doing extra takes to get a scene just right, whereas Tracy tended to get restless if a number of retakes kept him on the set longer than he had anticipated. Consequently it seemed improbable that Cukor and Tracy would ever relate well enough to each other professionally to make a picture together.

All such forecasts to the contrary, they got along beautifully during the making of *Keeper of the Flame.* Among other things, Tracy admired Cukor's knack for coping with Ms. Hepburn's manifold suggestions on how a scene should be played, especially the manner in which Cukor could satirically brush aside one of her ideas which he did not find helpful. While shooting a scene in which a building catches fire, Hepburn pointed out that she did not think the people in the area would have to be warned about the spread of the conflagration because they could smell the smoke. Cukor shot back that it must be wonderful for an actress "to know all about fires and all about acting too!"[8]

Tracy, unlike his costar, rarely conferred with Cukor about an upcoming scene. "Spence thought chewing over a scene with the director took all the magic out of it," Cukor explains. "He would think out how he was going to do a scene, and then he would just go ahead and do it. When I would look at the daily rushes the next day, however, everything that I *might* have suggested to him on the set the day before was right there in his performance in just the way that I wanted it. Spence was an intuitive actor who did not need a lot of 'hot tips' from me on how to interpret his part."

Like several other films in this chapter, *Keeper of the Flame* examines the attempt of individuals to reconcile their cherished dreams with the sober realities of life. Thus Ms. Hepburn plays Christine Forrest, a young woman who eventually pays the price for having tenaciously held on to her private illusions about her revered husband for far too long. Christine is the widow of a recently deceased political figure named Robert Forrest, whom reporter Steve O'Malley (Spencer Tracy) suspects was really a fanatic, madly conspiring at the time of his death to make himself the first dictator of the United States.

Christine does everything in her power to frustrate O'Malley's efforts to learn the truth about her husband, however, because she is laboring under the misapprehension that keeping the flame of Robert Forrest's spurious greatness alive can somehow serve as a continuing inspiration to his erstwhile followers who still idolize his memory. It is a measure of Cukor's subtlety as a director that he has permeated the film with visual metaphors about the concealing of truth. The tall trees that surround the Forrest estate, for example, signify the way that Forrest had succeeded during his lifetime in keeping the public at large from seeing the real Forrest through the trees.

The iron gate which O'Malley encounters the first time he ventures to visit the Forrest preserve, furthermore, prefigures how Christine will try to bar him from finding out about Forrest's treasonous conspiracy to take over the government. The shadowy room in which Christine first receives the reporter is another indication of her intent to keep these facts shrouded in darkness.

Once O'Malley discovers tucked away in the woods near the Forrest mansion the compound where the late demented leader secretly carried on his traitorous activities, he convinces Christine that Forrest's corrosive influence on his devotees will continue to do harm if she does not expose him to the world for what he was. In doing so, however, she pays with her life at the hands of Clive Spencer, one of Forrest's fiercely loyal henchmen. By becoming a martyr to the cause of truth, then, the misguided, though deeply sincere Christine becomes the feminine Christ figure that her name has all along implied that she might be. The crazed Spencer also puts a torch to Forrest's private hideaway; and as the film ends, the myth of Robert Forrest's greatness goes up in smoke along with all of the memorabilia that had been intended to keep his memory alive.

The dark, brooding atmosphere that permeates *Keeper of the Flame* marks it, of course, as an example of *film noir*, akin to other Cukor films of the period like *A Double Life* (1947). But Donald Stewart's screenplay was also an attack on the radical Right, as embodied in Robert Forrest's fascist cult; and during production both Tracy and Hepburn expressed misgivings that the political implications of the script were too overt for what was, after all, supposed to be primarily an entertaining thriller.

Looking back on the movie, Stewart has said, "This was the picture I was proudest of doing." By the 1940s, he explained, "we writers wanted to say something in pictures. It was, I think, partly guilt; but we had a feeling that it wasn't just entertainment that we had an obligation to provide. The story goes that Louis B. Mayer hadn't seen *Keeper of the Flame* until he went to a screening at the Radio City Music Hall, and he got up and walked out. I hope it's true."[9] It is.

To Mayer and others the film's explicit denunciation of the Right veered too much toward implicitly promoting the Left. My own judgment is that, despite Stewart's personally acknowledged leaning toward communism, the film's political sentiments are far too foggy to yield a precise political interpretation of any kind. Yet Stewart's screenplay for *Flame* was used as evidence against him during his appearance before the House Unamerican Activities Committee in 1951, as a result of which he was blacklisted from working in Hollywood and was forced to live and work in England, where he spent the balance of his life.

Neither at the time he made *Keeper of the Flame* nor at any time since has Cukor ever thought of the movie primarily as anything but a suspenseful psychological melodrama in which Katharine Hepburn gave one of her most nuanced performances, in a role that he has since termed her last really romantic "glamour girl" part. In subsequent films Ms. Hepburn was to depict no-nonsense characters who were more likely to help others face reality than to need that assistance themselves.

After *Keeper of the Flame* Cukor, Hepburn, and Tracy looked around for another property that they could film together. "Kate suggested that we could do the film version of Tennessee Williams's

The Glass Menagerie, with Laurette Taylor re-creating her stage
triumph as the mother, Kate as the daughter, and Spence as the girl's
Gentleman Caller." But unfortunately nothing came of the proposal
since a Hollywood producer had already bought the screen rights to
the play with another cast in mind.

Edward, My Son (1949)

It looked for a time that Cukor would again direct Tracy and
Hepburn, this time in Donald Stewart's screen adaptation of *Edward,
My Son*, based on the Robert Morley–Noel Langley play, which
Metro had acquired with a view to reuniting the director with the
acting team. Though Tracy did in fact play the male lead, British
actress Deborah Kerr convinced the front office that her floundering
American screen career could be rescued if the studio would allow
her to play the challenging role of Tracy's beleaguered wife. Hepburn
accompanied the unit to England, where the film was shot in the
summer and fall of 1948, however, and watched the filming. (*Edward,
My Son* incidentally, marked the first time in Cukor's career that he
made a movie outside the United States, though he was to travel as far
as India and Russia to do location work in the years to come.)

In *Edward, My Son* Spencer Tracy plays Arnold Boult, a man who
singlemindedly dedicates himself to giving his only son every advantage in life which he was denied. He ruthlessly destroys anyone who
stands in the way of his realizing this goal, including his hapless wife,
Evelyn, who tries unsuccessfully to keep her husband from turning
the lad into the worthless, spoiled lout that he eventually becomes.

Following the format of the play, Stewart's screenplay does not
permit Edward to appear on screen; but the constant references to
the young man in the dialogue enable the viewer to chart Edward's
decline. His father, of course, sees him quite differently than others
do; and the movie opens with Boult proudly telling the moviegoer
about his son.

This prologue, which follows immediately after the credits, begins
with the screen in darkness. In the distance a door opens, allowing a
shaft of light to pierce the blackness. Arnold Boult enters and walks
toward the camera. He speaks directly to the audience, asking them
to judge for themselves if he was not justified in subordinating
everyone and everything in his life to the welfare of his only son.
Throughout the course of the movie, the voice of Boult continues to
narrate the story on the sound track; and in the epilogue at the end of

the picture he appears once again in this same nondescript setting where the movie began to repeat his plea that the audience should not judge him harshly, since what he did was for Edward and not for himself.

Then he turns slowly away and exits through the door through which he had entered in the prologue, shutting it behind him and leaving the screen once more in darkness. Nevertheless, the audience has not been left in the dark about the true nature of Boult's unspeakable behavior as it has been depicted for them in the picture, regardless of how Boult has tried to explain it away.

This device of having the central character address himself to the audience worked well enough in the theater when Robert Morley, who created the role of Arnold Boult in the play, stepped to the front of the stage and talked to the people sitting in the auditorium in front of him. But the self-same technique seems to be a forced and artificial gimmick when transferred to the screen, since each moviegoer is aware that Tracy is addressing the camera on a movie set, and is really not present in the theater with him in the way that Morley was present to each theatergoer when he confided his tale to the latter on the other side of the footlights from him.

Nevertheless, if the particular method in which the prologue and epilogue were employed in the film of *Edward, My Son* smacks too much of the stage, Cukor sought in other ways to liberate the action from theatrical conventions. Like the play on which it is based, the film adaptation of *Edward, My Son* contains several prolonged dialogue scenes which could have been very static and stagey on the screen. Cukor got around this difficulty by filming these self-contained episodes in long takes in which he cleverly works his camera around the actors as it unobtrusively glides about the set, so that the pace of the action never falters. He "cuts inside the camera" by closing in at times for a close shot to emphasize a key gesture or capture a significant facial expression, then falling back for a medium or long shot as the action continues. Because Cukor rarely opted to interrupt these long takes by the insertion of other shots, he virtually eliminated the need for any editing in these particular scenes when the footage was cut together.

Cukor had used this technique of cutting inside the camera as early as *Rockabye* (1932), but never before as effectively as in *Edward, My Son*, especially in the crucial sequence in which Boult and his wife quarrel bitterly about Edward's future plans. The camera follows Arnold and Evelyn as they pace around the room hurling mutual recriminations at each other. When Evelyn at last submits once more to her husband's overpowering personality, the camera holds on both of them while she staggers away from him and falls into a crushed heap on the bed. Their relative distance from the camera at this point symbolically defines the relationship of tyrannical domination and abject submission that exists between them: Arnold remains an imposing figure in the foreground of the shot, while Evelyn has sunk into insignificance in the background, where she languishes on the bed sobbing helplessly and hopelessly.

All in all, Cukor's experimentation with long takes in *Edward, My Son* was every bit as skillfully done as Hitchcock's had been in *Rope* a year earlier. But as usual Cukor concealed his technical craftsmanship by making the camerawork seem so effortless that hardly anyone noticed the infinite care with which these prolonged takes were executed, though Hitchcock's similar employment of this device in *Rope* was much examined and discussed by the critics as an interesting tour de force.

Deborah Kerr was widely praised for her portrayal of Evelyn Boult, but Tracy was miscast as Arnold Boult. It is true that Cukor had successfully cast matinee idols Charles Boyer and Ronald Colman against type as mad murderers in *Gaslight* (1944) and *A Double Life* (1947), respectively; but Tracy's screen image as an essentially good-natured kind of person was simply too firmly fixed in the minds of the mass audience to allow them to accept him as a vicious neurotic in *Edward, My Son*. In addition, because he was not accustomed to playing such a completely unsympathetic role, Tracy did not bring that degree of conviction to the part which would have made his performance totally credible.

Withal, *Edward, My Son* is a gripping melodrama that merits rediscovery, as much for Cukor's intricate camerawork as for the superb characterizations by Deborah Kerr and the strong supporting cast, most of whom were recruited from the original stage production.

Edward, My Son was the last of eight Cukor films on which Donald Ogden Stewart worked over the years, for he was soon to be blacklisted, as noted above. His other credits on Cukor pictures include *Holiday, The Philadelphia Story*, and *Keeper of the Flame*, all discussed in this chapter; plus *Tarnished Lady, Dinner at Eight, A Woman's Face*, and (uncredited) *The Women*.

Cukor's next film after *Edward, My Son, Adam's Rib*, was written by the husband and wife team of Garson Kanin and Ruth Gordon, who together or separately were involved in creating an equal number of screenplays for Cukor.

Adam's Rib (1949)

Besides *Adam's Rib*, Garson Kanin and Ruth Gordon also coauthored *A Double Life*, *The Marrying Kind*, and *Pat and Mike*; Ruth Gordon adapted *The Actress* from her own play *Years Ago*; Garson Kanin wrote the screenplay of *It Should Happen to You*, and (uncredited) was principally responsible for the film adaptation of his play *Born Yesterday*. The Kanins, along with Donald Ogden Stewart, then, constitute the talents to whom Cukor most frequently turned for material.

For a director, the next best thing to writing his own scripts is to be able to work with writers whose screenplays are congenial to his directorial style and personal vision. Yet Cukor says that he did not systematically single out certain screen writers to provide him with a significant number of scripts during his long career: "You don't think to yourself, 'Well, it's time to do my next Kanin script,' or anything like that. You only realize with hindsight how often you have used the same writers, because a director just works from one picture to the next according to what's available at the time he is casting about for his next project." In the case of *Adam's Rib*, Cukor chose to film the Kanins' original screenplay because it seemed made to order for Tracy and Hepburn; and Cukor was itching to direct them again after the indifferent success of *Keeper of the Flame*.

An established actress in her own right, Ruth Gordon had first encountered Cukor at his Rochester summer-stock company back in the 1920s, and had later appeared in his film *Two-Faced Woman* (1941). For his part, Garson Kanin had himself directed worthy films like *My Favorite Wife* (1940). Hence the Kanins' combined experience in acting and directing proved a considerable asset when they turned to constructing screenplays.

The original title of the film under discussion was to have been *Man and Wife*; but the authors altered that to *Adam's Rib* (not to be confused with C. B. DeMille's 1923 comedy of the same title about flappers), and likewise changed the male lead's name from Ned to Adam in order to make a playful allusion to the Book of Genesis.

While the screenplay was still in preparation, Cukor followed his usual custom of holding script conferences with the writers in order to trade ideas about plot and dialogue. "I'm not a writer," he comments;

"but I know how to hector screenwriters and make suggestions that will help them improve what they have written. To that extent I am more of a critic than a collaborator where the script is concerned." Even after production had begun on *Adam's Rib* and the Kanins had gone on to other projects, Cukor would phone them from time to time and ask for revisions in a scene which had read well on paper but was not playing well when acted out on the set. They would invariably oblige by phoning him back in a few hours with additional dialogue that was just what the director ordered.

In *Adam's Rib* Katharine Hepburn enacts a canny lawyer named Amanda Bonner who is defending Doris Attinger (Judy Holliday), a young woman accused of the attempted murder of her philandering husband, Warren (Tom Ewell). Amanda's husband, Adam (Spencer Tracy), as Warren's attorney, steadfastly tries to keep Amanda from escalating the case into a crusade for women's rights; and this proves to be quite a challenge.

In order to establish at the outset that the film represents yet one more skirmish in the age-old battle of the sexes, the opening credits appear on the curtain of a Punch and Judy stage. To reinforce the comic parallel between the contentious Bonners and the legendary figures of Punch and Judy, moreover, Cukor stages one scene in the Bonner bedroom as if it were part of a Punch and Judy show: he photographs the whole sequence with a stationary camera which frames the action as if it were taking place on a Punch and Judy stage, with the quarreling Bonners entering and exiting from opposite sides of the screen as if they were going on and off stage.

The Punch and Judy symbolism is capped in the film's final scene, in which Adam and Amanda are once more reconciled to each other. They are sitting on a fourposter bed, and at the fade-out Adam draws the curtain of the fourposter across the bed as if he were closing the curtain on a Punch and Judy stage at the end of a performance.

The studied theatricality of the movie's Punch and Judy imagery is offset by Cukor's highly cinematic use of locations throughout the film. There is a documentary air about the opening scene in which the camera follows Doris as she in turn follows her husband across town to his assignation with his mistress. It is a brilliant stroke to have Doris boning up on the instructions for firing a revolver from a gun manual while she stands in the corridor outside the mistress's shabby flat before she bursts in, spraying bullets in all directions.

The courtroom scenes also have the authentic flavor of a documentary. A stickler for accuracy of detail in his films, Cukor toured

Katharine Hepburn consults with Judy Holliday in Adam's Rib *(1949), Miss Holliday's first important film.*

New York courtrooms with Ms. Hepburn prior to the beginning of production in order to watch actual trials in progress.

One of the most riveting sequences occurs in the women's house of detention, where Amanda interviews Doris for the first time. Cukor decided to shoot the scene in one 7½-minute take, despite the fact that Ms. Holliday had had little screen experience up to this point in her acting career. Many a more seasoned actress would have balked at attempting to hold a movie audience's attention for so long a span of screen time. But Cukor had a hunch that she could carry it off with Ms. Hepburn's help, and so she did. While Ms. Hepburn looked on, Ms. Holliday played to the camera the entire time and delivered a beautifully sustained performance.

"It was said that Judy stole that scene from Kate, but that is nonsense," comments Cukor. "Scene stealing implies that a performer deliberately draws attention to himself just to show off. But Kate willingly gave the scene away to Judy because the story demanded that the audience's attention be focused more on Judy's character at this point than on Kate's." (As already noted, John

Barrymore did Ms. Hepburn the same favor when they were shooting *Bill of Divorcement* back in 1932.)

The climax of the film occurs, not when Amanda wins the case for
Doris, but when Adam persuades Amanda by a crafty ruse that Doris
was really not justified in shooting her husband. Adam threatens to
kill Amanda when he finds her in the company of another man. After
she insists that Adam has no right to shoot her, he nonchalantly puts
the weapon into his mouth and bends the barrel with his teeth: the
"gun" is made of licorice. This is the perfect payoff for an inventive,
inspired farce, possibly the best film that Tracy and Hepburn ever
made together.

Pat and Mike (1952)

Pat and Mike was the last of the three Cukor films in which Tracy
and Hepburn costarred. The basic concept of *Pat and Mike* occurred
to Garson Kanin after watching Katharine Hepburn in a tennis
match. He told his wife, Ruth Gordon, that it would be interesting to
devise a screenplay for Tracy and Hepburn in which Pat, a lady
athlete from an upper-class background, would fall in love with a
crude but lovable promoter à la Damon Runyon.

Cukor recalls that his first runthrough of the script with the two
principals and the two writers took place in his home, and that
everyone present was astonished at the way Tracy transformed himself into Mike so convincingly during this preliminary reading. Garson Kanin has said that, as Tracy sat in a corner of the room reading his
lines with his eye glasses perched on the end of his nose, the character
of Mike came to life right in their midst, complete with a three-
dimensional personality far more real than the one he and his cos-
cenarist had imagined.[10]

In the course of training Pat to be an all-round champion athlete,
Mike eventually wins her away from her buttoned-down, uptight
fiancé, Collier Weld, whose overbearing personality has for too long
stifled her spirit and sapped her self-esteem by his constantly badger-
ing her about her supposed inadequacies. Early in the movie, when
Pat appears dressed in slacks for a golf date with him, the fastidious
Collier insists that she change into a skirt, subconsciously suggesting
that he alone will wear the pants in the Weld family once he and Pat
are married. Furthermore, he registers his disapproval of Pat's
changing into a skirt in the back seat of his open sports car on the way
to the golf links by prudishly adjusting the rear-view mirror so that he

cannot see her doing so. Not surprisingly, by the time that they reach the country club, Pat is too ill-at-ease to play very well; and then Collier scolds her for being off her game.

Mike, on the other hand, respects Pat not only as an athlete but as a woman; and therein lies the deep foundation of the mutual feeling that gradually springs up between these two unlikely lovers. Because Pat and Mike seem so mismatched on the surface, Cukor depicts their relationship as taking shape very slowly; and its growth is subtly documented by remarks that are tossed off almost as casual asides by each of them, as well as by the most guarded gestures of endearment.

Mike registers his initial attraction for Pat between gulps of water from a drinking fountain by muttering, "Nicely packed, that kid. There's not much meat on her, but what's there is cherce." At another point, after Pat bestows a discreet peck on Mike's cheek, he makes a show of wiping the kiss away with his handkerchief; and then shyly pockets the handkerchief as a keepsake.

The romantic dimension of the plot is played against the background of professional sporting events, and Cukor had at his disposal several famous athletes to act as technical advisers on the film and to participate in the game sequences. One of them was tennis pro Bill Tilden, whose description of how an athlete feels when he is not playing well formed the basis of a delightful fantasy sequence. As Pat begins to lose a tennis match, the net suddenly grows to a staggering height and her tennis racket shrinks to the size of a spoon.

Although the dialogue in *Pat and Mike* is not up to the best verbal volleys in *Adam's Rib*, Tracy and Hepburn's expert teamwork, coupled with Cukor's customary grace and polish in handling lightweight material of this kind, adds up to a pleasantly zany comedy. Indeed, Pauline Kael has written that *Pat and Mike*, along with *Adam's Rib*, make some of the other films in which Tracy and Hepburn were paired look like warm-ups by comparison.[11] It is a pity that, although Cukor would direct each of them in other movies, Tracy and Hepburn never again appeared together in a Cukor film.

The Actress (1953)

Tracy's last picture for Cukor was *The Actress*, which Ruth Gordon adapted from her autobiographical play about her youth entitled *Years Ago*. Ms. Hepburn was in fact offered the role of the young Ruth's mother, opposite Tracy as the girl's father; but she decided instead to return to the stage in a revival of Shaw's *Millionairess*, and the role went to Teresa Wright. Jean Simmons was cast as Ruth Jones, the young Ruth Gordon. "It was the only time that I have ever seen a British-born actress play an American girl with absolute authenticity," says Cukor. "She's a wonderfully gifted actress."

As part of the preproduction preliminaries, Cukor and Ruth Gordon visited her hometown of Wollaston, Massachusetts, to do background research for the movie. "We visited the house where Ruth grew up," Cukor recalls; "and we took several pictures of the old homestead to help the art director design the sets." Cukor was particularly fascinated by the kitchen, which unaccountably had no less than six doors. "No art director could have dreamed up that kitchen," says Cukor. "It had the texture of reality about it, and it looked very genuine when we reproduced it on the sound stage back at MGM." To keep within the film's modest budget, the exteriors were shot in Pasadena, California, rather than in Massachusetts; but so painstaking was the research done by Cukor and his staff before filming began that few filmgoers guessed that the picture was not shot on location in New England.

The Actress revolves around the relationship of Ruth and her flinty, yet essentially warmhearted father, whom she must convince to let her try her luck at an acting career in New York. As Clinton Jones, Tracy gives one of the best and most understated performances of his entire career. He is especially touching in the scene in which Jones's resolve to keep his daughter from migrating to New York City begins to give way in the face of his daughter's determination.

When Cukor complimented Tracy on his handling of this scene, the latter replied, "Well, I remember when I told my father that I wanted to be an actor, he looked at me, this skinny kid with big ears, and he said, 'Oh, that poor little son-of-a-bitch; he's going to go through an awful lot.'"[12] Garson Kanin adds that Tracy often quoted the advice he once received from George M. Cohan about the acting profession: "Whatever you do, kid, always serve it with a little dressing."[13] Tracy's drawing on his memories of his own father provided just the right amount of "dressing" to enable Tracy to serve up this particular scene in the film to perfection.

Interestingly enough, Cukor made use of his own boyhood recollections while making *The Actress*. The opening sequence, which shows Ruth watching a stage show from the higher reaches of the gallery, nostalgically recalls the many hours which the young Cukor, like the stagestruck Ruth Jones, spent in theater balconies, entranced by the theatrical greats of the day. The first musical comedy that she sneaked up to Boston to see, Ruth Gordon recalls, was *The Pink Lady*, featuring Hazel Dawn as a wicked Parisian siren stunningly decked out in spangles and crowned with pink Bird of Paradise feathers in her hair. "All I wanted out of a career," says Ms. Gordon wistfully, "was to look like Hazel Dawn and wear pink feathers."[14]

In the first scene in the film Cukor photographs a sumptuous production number from *The Pink Lady* from Ruth Jones's point of view in the second balcony. The shimmering chandelier over the stage seems to reflect Ruth's own inner glow as she becomes swept up in the breathtaking spectacle spread out before her on the brightly lit stage below. (During the movie's first-run engagements, movie houses around the country that were equipped to do so projected this opening sequence of the movie in wide screen to lend it an added grandeur.)

In a later scene Ruth absentmindedly hums this same waltz from *The Pink Lady* as her beau (Anthony Perkins, in his first film) leaves the house—"one of the recurrent signs that her mind is on show business," and not on boyfriends, as Douglas McVay writes.[15] The melody surges forth on the sound track one last time in the film's finale as Mr. and Mrs. Jones leave the house with Ruth to accompany her to the railway station for her trip to New York. The camera remains inside the house, photographing their departure through the parlor window. The trio are last seen retreating down the street in the distance, as if they are disappearing into the past and equivalently returning to the pages of the family album in which they were enshrined during the movie's main title sequence.

In shooting the extended dialogue sequences in *The Actress*, Cukor favored long, unbroken takes similar to those which he employed in *Edward, My Son*. "A scene has to be well written and well played to sustain the audience's interest throughout a long take," he explains. "So I only use long takes when I'm sure both the screenplay and the actors are up to it." That was clearly the case in *The Actress*.

The movie is in essence a straightforward, unsentimental depiction of family life which stringently avoids being banal and folksy. It is a great pity, therefore, that the producers did not leave well enough alone instead of softening the central character's personality by snipping out some footage in which she manifested the tough, ambitious side of her nature. As Cukor sees Ruth Jones, she represents the kind of young people who realize that they need to be unswerving, not to say ruthless, in pursuing cherished goals if they are really serious about achieving them. "Ruth certainly was such a person," he concludes; "otherwise she wouldn't have had the gumption to leave home in the first place." *The Actress* was not the first or the last Cukor film to be tampered with by producers, and it is a tribute to his direction that *The Actress* still holds up despite this kind of studio interference.

Love Among the Ruins (1975)

As a kind of coda to their parallel careers, Cukor and Hepburn have done two television films together, the first of which was *Love Among the Ruins* (not to be confused with the Evelyn Waugh novelette of the same title), first telecast by ABC-TV March 6, 1975. James Costigan had originally conceived the story as a theatrical vehicle for Alfred Lunt and Lynn Fontanne, who ultimately decided to retire from the stage instead of doing another play. The author then rewrote the script as a teleplay and submitted it to Katharine Hepburn, who liked it enough to send it on to Cukor, who in turn was also enthusiastic about it. The director then invited Laurence Olivier to costar with Ms. Hepburn.

His first day on the set Cukor asked the producer, "How does one shoot for television? Should I do a lot more close-ups for the smaller screen than I would normally do for a theatrical film, or what?" The latter advised the director to shoot the telefilm in the same way that he would direct a theatrical feature. "So that's what I did," says Cukor. "I had a vague notion that I was making the film for the tube, and that hence I shouldn't overload the frame with too much detail at any one time. But in actual fact I didn't have to modify my directorial style very much at all, since, after all, there weren't any big, epic sequences such as battle scenes in the story that required a cast of thousands; most of the action took place in a courtroom."

The telefilm was shot in London, and when Cukor returned to California after the completion of principal photography, he wrote to me that the experience of working with Hepburn and Olivier "was a most harmonious and happy one. I'm hoping that the results will show our relish in making the film."[16] Cukor got his wish.

In *Love Among the Ruins* Sir Arthur Granville-Jones, an elderly barrister (Laurence Olivier), defends Jessica Medlicott (Katharine Hepburn), a wealthy retired actress, in a breach-of-promise suit brought against her by a young gold digger named Alfred Pratt. Sir Arthur has secretly idolized Jessica ever since they shared a brief youthful fling many years before; and the first time that she appears in his office to discuss the case, she is enveloped in the rays of the late-afternoon sun streaming through a window still sparkling with raindrops from a recent shower. In this dazzling atmosphere it seems to Arthur that a radiant apparition of the inaccessible goddess whom he has worshiped these many years has suddenly materialized before him.

Though he is probably unaware of it, the vehemence with which he defends Jessica in court partially stems from his personal animosity toward the young plaintiff, whom he sees as totally unworthy of this lady whom he has himself loved these many years. As Carlos Clarens puts it, Olivier manages to cram into his portrayal of Sir Arthur both "the anxiety of first love and the exasperation of old age."

Arthur wins the case with the aid of Jessica's shrewd courtroom play acting, by means of which she passes herself off to the jury as a foolish and erratic old woman easily taken in by an opportunistic young bounder. And Arthur wins Jessica as well, thus bringing into relief the telefilm's title, a satirical reference to the advanced age of the two lovers, drawn from Browning's poem of the same title about the ruins of classical antiquity.

But by this time, Arthur's having had to cope with this feisty and unpredictable woman throughout the arduous trial has worn away his idealized vision of her as the ethereal creature of his dreams; and he is prepared to accept her as the flesh-and-blood creature that she really is. Once more a Cukor character is forced to trade in his fantasies for a less glamorous but more substantial reality. In the final scene, "the once and future lovers," as Clarens calls them, walk arm in arm out of the courthouse into the cheerful sunshine.[17] Though they have both reached the autumn of life, the renewal of their love has made them feel, in the exhilaration of the moment, younger than springtime. And one is reminded of another poem of Browning's, "Rabbi Ben Ezra," which begins, "Grow old along with me! / The best is yet to be."

Love Among the Ruins swept the Emmys for 1975, winning awards for the director, both costars, the scriptwriter, and production designer Carmen Dillon. Even the modest Cukor is prepared to concede that this was not a bad showing for a production that began with the director inquiring of the producer how one went about shooting a film for television. "I was working with two bums, Hepburn and Olivier," Cukor adds with a wink; "and in spite of them I did all right."

An epochal event: Katharine Hepburn, George Cukor (in background) and Lord Laurence Olivier in Cukor's first telefilm, Love Among the Ruins *(1975), for which all three carried off Emmy Awards.*

The Corn Is Green (1979)

The Corn Is Green, first telecast by CBS-TV January 29, 1979, was the tenth Cukor-Hepburn film and their second for television, actually a remake of the 1945 motion picture starring Bette Davis. The project got off the ground when Cukor phoned Ms. Hepburn to tell her that Alan Shayne, head of Warners-TV, wanted them both to do *The Corn Is Green*. In examining the script Ms. Hepburn was just as impressed as Cukor was with the story of Lily C. Moffat, the spirited spinster who takes in hand the training of Morgan Evans, an intelligent youth working in a Welsh mine, so that he can win a scholarship to Oxford. Their relationship is a rocky one, because Morgan is just as strong-willed as his mentor; but they nevertheless succeed in their mutual endeavor and reach a mutual understanding in the bargain. Like the unripened corn of the title, Morgan grows to maturity with the help of her careful cultivation, and reaps the harvest that their combined efforts deserve.

Both director and star found L. C. Moffat a fascinating character. "She is not grim and schoolmarmish like so many modern feminists," Cukor explains. "There is a definite lack of humor and charm in the women's liberation movement today," and ladies like Lily Moffat illustrate that a woman can be intelligent and independent without ceasing to be warm and human. She can, for example, comment on her status as an elderly unmarried woman without a trace of self-pity. "If you still are a spinster by the time you are thirty," she muses, "you realize that the gentleman you've been waiting for has lost his way and isn't coming. So you might as well enjoy life." It is understandable why Cukor and Hepburn wanted to bring to life such an engaging character on the home screen.

Cukor accordingly put together a production package that reunited most of the Emmy winners of *Love Among the Ruins.* Besides Ms. Hepburn and himself, there was Carmen Dillon to design the sets and James Costigan to adapt Emlyn Williams's play for TV (though Costigan ultimately substituted the pseudonym of "Ivan Davis" in the screen credits for his own name because of disagreements over script changes).

Cukor agreed with Ms. Hepburn that the exteriors should be photographed on location in Wales. "You pick up the indefinable when you go to the source," she has written in an article about the production, because the climate and the terrain affects a performer's interpretation of a role. She and Cukor toured the Welsh countryside scouting location sites for the telefilm, and selected for L. C. Moffat's cottage a farmhouse called Hafod Ifan. It was Carmen Dillon's personal choice as well, and she indicated to director and star "how she could build on here and there, and make the property fit the script."[18] When the shooting in Wales was finished, the unit moved on to a London studio to film the interiors.

It was obvious throughout the production period that, since Cukor and Hepburn had been working together for nearly half a century, each of them could by this time almost intuit what the other had in mind about the way a given scene should be played. And of course their deeply rooted mutual respect never wavered, despite occasional disagreements. "He has plenty of opinions, and he's constantly saying things that stimulate you," Ms. Hepburn remarked about Cukor during shooting; "but he gives his actors freedom. He doesn't shut them into a trap, like some directors who push their actors around like dolls."

"Yes, she is full of ideas, and most of them extremely good; of course I try her patience and she tries mine," Cukor countered. "But there's a complete absence of sham and nonsense between us. A real rapport." That rapport was evidenced by the flippant banter that punctuated their dealings on the set. "Ms. Hepburn's holding us up again," Cukor would cry in simulated irritation. "She's always doing that," the actress would reply, fully aware that she was doing no such thing, given the fact that she was usually letter-perfect in her lines and therefore required few retakes.[19]

Two weeks before the premiere telecast, Cukor said in a letter, "We've been having several previews of *The Corn Is Green*. Happily they've been going very well."[20] When the telefilm was aired, television reviewers complimented Cukor's staging of the story against the lush Welsh landscapes as well as Ms. Hepburn's commanding screen presence. In the course of the film, moreover, the director demonstrated that his eye for visual symbols was still as acute as ever. For example, the first time that Morgan (Ian Saynor) meets Lily Moffat formally, he stands on the road outside her cottage and diffidently converses with her through the window, signaling that he is as yet hesitant to enter her world of culture and knowledge by coming inside.

On the negative side, *Time* wondered why the original play was not opened out for the TV screen more than it was. "When Morgan Evans travels up to Oxford to take his exams, the audience expects to go with him," *Time* noted; but they are left behind in Wales with Lily Moffat.[21] For my money, Cukor was wise to keep his camera trained on Ms. Moffat back home as she frets about Morgan's ordeal at Oxford. Essentially *The Corn Is Green* is not, after all, about the lad's struggle to rise above his grim and grimy background, but about the rejuvenation which his mentor experiences in helping him do so.

Hence Morgan's ultimate success at Oxford in winning the coveted scholarship is all the more rewarding for the audience when they learn about it at the same time that Lily does, and can consequently share her sense of relief and joy, just as they shared her anxiety about him all the time he was away. In Cukor's own words, "The construction of the whole story was around Lily and not the boy. I thought the scene in which Morgan comes back and tells her all about what happened to him was eloquently written and very effective." Never one to mince words when discussing his work, he adds, "With all due respect to all those marvelous playwrights on the staff of *Time*, in this particular instance I don't think they know what the hell they are talking about."

In summarizing this chapter, one can say that Cukor obviously enjoyed a symbiotic relationship with Tracy and Hepburn, whether he was directing them separately or as a team. Their professional relationship was matched by the lasting friendship that the trio enjoyed in private. In the 1930s Cukor built a couple of small guest houses in the lower garden of his estate; and Spencer Tracy lived in one of them for about twenty years, until his death in 1967. He was succeeded by Ms. Hepburn, who lived there for ten years, until she took up residence in recent years in New York City. "They were both good tenants," Cukor says puckishly; "they always paid their rent on time."

Asked about the close personal relationship of Tracy and Hepburn, the director replies, "Whatever their relationship off screen, it enriched their work on screen." Since they were two of the foremost actors of their generation, he continues, "they were wonderful ensemble players who worked harmoniously with each other and with me."

As I remarked at the beginning of this chapter, Katharine Hepburn is the first to acknowledge her debt to Cukor for the influence he has had on her career from the start. In her article about *The Corn Is Green* she recalls a phone conversation with Cukor in which she teased him by saying, "Yes, George, I know you made me what I am. No, I won't forget. You won't let me."[22] She expressed her regard for Cukor more seriously at the Lincoln Center tribute to the director when she said, "I did my first film with George. I hope *The Corn Is Green* won't be my last."[23]

One can easily share those sentiments.

4

Fair Ladies:
Legendary Actresses

"WHEN I CAME TO HOLLYWOOD FROM THE NEW YORK THEATER," Cukor recalls, "everyone immediately typed me as a New York sophisticate"; and critics and film historians have been trying to type Cukor ever since. Because he came to movieland from Broadway, he has been said to make films that are more theatrical than cinematic in technique, a criticism that I have hopefully laid to rest in Chapter 2. Because leading actresses of the screen like Katharine Hepburn (see Chapter 3) and those to be considered in this chapter have excelled under his direction, he has been called a woman's director—a label he particularly dislikes. "There were men in those movies along with the ladies," he notes laconically.

Indeed there were, and Cukor has directed males like James Stewart, Ronald Colman, and Rex Harrison, as well as females like Ingrid Bergman and Judy Holliday, in Oscar-winning performances. Without wishing in any way to slight Cukor's work with males, it is still well worth exploring in this chapter a group of pictures which exemplify the string of undeniably superior performances he has drawn from several extraordinary actresses, including Garbo, Crawford, and Holliday. (The Cukor films starring the equally legendary Harlow, Garland, Bergman, and Monroe are for a variety of reasons treated in other parts of this book.)

Cukor feels that he got pigeonholed as a woman's director because he hit his stride as a director in the days when the great movie queens like Garbo and Crawford were flourishing. Furthermore, as Allan Estrin suggests in his section on Cukor in his *Hollywood Professionals* volume, Cukor had a way of coaxing each of these female superstars into submerging their stereotyped screen personalities in the roles that they played in his pictures, so that more often than not they gave better performances for Cukor than for other directors.

Cukor directing Garbo in Camille *(1937), her greatest film.*

Garbo's portrayal of the central role in *Camille* (1937) is a case in point, for under Cukor's direction she does not merely play Camille; she inhabits the role.

Garbo and *Camille* (1937)

By the mid-1930s Cukor had reached the point in his career when he was able to select the subjects which he wanted to film. When he was invited to direct a Garbo picture at this time, therefore, he was offered a choice between *The Lady of the Camellias* (better known as *Camille*) by Alexandre Dumas *fils* and *Marie Walewska,* a costume drama built around Napoleon and his mistress of that name. He rejected the latter (later directed by Clarence Brown under the title *Conquest*) because he has always shied away from trying to bring actual historical figures to life on the screen. "They always seem to me to have been borrowed from a wax works," he explains.

Furthermore, Cukor preferred *Camille* to *Marie* because he had a hunch that *Camille* would represent the perfect meeting of an actress with a role she was destined to play. His surmise proved to be absolutely correct, for in *Camille* Garbo delivered what is surely the best performance of her entire career. (*Conquest,* on the other hand, was not well received.)

Pauline Kael has written that since Metro publicists crowed in 1931 that in *Anna Christie* "Garbo talks!" they could have just as proudly proclaimed that in *Camille* "Garbo acts!" In the latter film Garbo plays a courtesan named Marguerite Gauthier who is "too intelligent for her frivolous life, too generous for her circumstances," Ms. Kael continues. "It's a sublime, ironic performance."[1] Under Cukor's assured direction the actress transforms a film that might have been a standard tear-jerker into the classic motion picture the studio hoped it would be.

Camille had been filmed no less than six times during the silent era, notably in 1912 with Bernhardt and in 1921 with Alla Nazimova and Rudolph Valentino in the leads. Consequently Cukor was concerned that the creaky plot mechanics of Dumas's old-fashioned nineteenth-century melodrama would not be too apparent in his sound version of this familiar tale. His misgivings were allayed, however, when he saw the final shooting script prepared by Zoë Akins, whose story *Girls About Town* Cukor had filmed in 1931. She had wisely scuttled the earlier draft of the screenplay done by some other writers and started from page one to do her own version. "Zoë had a fine sense of style," says Cukor; her script was completely free of the dated dialogue and sentimental kitsch that characterized the original play.

As the story of *Camille* unfolds, Marguerite, already aware that she is dying of tuberculosis, falls in love with Armand Duval, a young diplomat (Robert Taylor). Marguerite desperately wants to make the most of the love that she shares with Armand for as long as she can, and so she gives up the night life of Paris to live in a country cottage with him. But their idyllic interlude is doomed to be shortlived; and, like many another Cukor character, Camille is made to face this agonizing reality when she enters upon her last illness.

Camille's death scene proves beyond a doubt that Garbo was a consummate actress as well as a paragon of beauty. In anticipation of Armand's appearance, she wears a corsage of her beloved camellias and summons all of her meager strength to greet him joyously. But as Armand lifts her up in an embrace, Marguerite's life already seems to be slipping away from her. When he tells her that they will return to the country where her health will revive, we know that Marguerite can no longer hold on to this illusion, much as she would like to. "Perhaps it's better if I live in your heart, where the world can't see me," she says; then an ecstatic smile fills her face, and she expires. Thus does this timeless romance conclude precisely as it should, Bosley Crowther comments, "with the ideal, illusory woman still lovely and imperishable, in a bereft man's arms."[2]

Speaking of this, the last scene in the film, Cukor says, "Garbo went through a great deal to get a scene right. I once told her that she seemed to act so easily; and she laughed and said that she would kill me for saying that," because she worked out every gesture in advance and learned every syllable of dialogue exactly as written. "She never improvised," Cukor continues; "and I respected her for this. I am a great believer in following the text to the letter because improvised dialogue has no well-defined tempo; it is slipshod and invariably makes the scene seem listless. For me improvising on the set is always a disaster. The real trick is to make the scene look as if it were improvised by giving the performance a sense of spontaneity. To accomplish this you must know how much to rehearse an actor, so as not to overdo it and make the scene go stale. The proper amount of rehearsing does not diminish the freshness of a given scene, however, but rather enriches the scene. When the moment of creation comes on the set, things will begin to happen the way you want them to if the scene has been carefully prepared."

One scene which Garbo rehearsed with intense concentration, but which comes across on the screen with great spontaneity, occurs in the film after Marguerite has made up her mind not to see Armand again in order not to spoil his young life. Just as Sydney Fairchild in *Bill of Divorcement* (1932) joins her father at the keyboard to drown out the sound of her former fiancé's call to join him in the yard outside, so, too, Marguerite listens to Baron de Varville, one of her clients (Henry Danielle), play the piano in order to distract herself from hearing Armand frantically ringing her doorbell. Marguerite laughs raucously all the while, displaying a gaiety that can only be a painful pretense. In the light of this sequence, Cukor is still mystified by the fuss that Metro later made in their ad campaign for *Ninotchka* (1939), proudly declaring it as the film in which "Garbo laughs!"— since she surely laughed in *Camille*.

Camille was the last film to be supervised by Irving Thalberg as chief of production at MGM. After Thalberg died, Eddie Mannix, a studio executive, phoned Cukor and said, "Since *Camille* is Irving's last picture, is there anything you would like to do to improve it?" "Really, it's not necessary," Cukor replied; "but, yes, I suppose I could do a little retouching." So he shot for an additional three days to refine a scene or two as a token of his abiding personal esteem for Thalberg, whom he still regards as "the most brilliant, the most creative producer that I ever worked with. That includes *everyone*."[3]

Robert Taylor often said that *Camille* was one of his favorites among his own films, because it represents one of the finest performances of his career. "Cukor is an expert at bringing out the best in actors," he explained.[4] Yet the initial reviews of the film in the trade papers were largely negative, and for the most curious reason.

"There is a custom in Hollywood that directors and stars should advertise themselves in the trade press from time to time," says Cukor. "I consistently refused to do this, so the trade press got after me and dismissed *Camille*. But it went on to become a popular picture, and over the years has become something of a distinguished film. Yet it is not my favorite film; I'm against categorizing my films in this fashion. I always tend to lean toward a film that has left some impact on the viewer in several scenes, even if it is not a great film in one's overall judgment. A picture that has failed can still have some extraordinary scenes in it; but because the story doesn't carry the picture as a whole, the film is not a success." Such a film was *Sylvia Scarlett* (1936). And such a film was *Two-Faced Woman*, Cukor's other Garbo movie.

Two-Faced Woman (1941)

Two-Faced Woman, which turned out to be Garbo's last picture, had some excellent bits of farce in it, but otherwise was a disappointment. "It was a novel idea to have Garbo play a woman who pretends to be twins," Cukor remarks; "but we started shooting before the screenplay was really ready. I have often said that, if I am given a good script, I will be a hundred times better as a director. The reason is that you have to use every possible artifice and subterfuge to bolster a weak script; and in the end the strain always shows in the finished film, as it did in this one."

Another reason *Two-Faced Woman* failed was that Garbo's personality was not attuned to playing a part that really called for a thoroughgoing comedienne, something which this statuesque creature could never be. Garbo had been able to bring off the comedy in *Ninotchka* two years earlier because, as Gary Carey perceptively points out, much of the comedy in that film was predicated on the fact that the solemn heroine lacked a sense of humor. In the present film, however, Garbo was manifestly miscast in a lighthearted role for which she was fundamentally unsuited. By contrast, Ruth Gordon (in one of her first screen appearances) and Constance Bennett (who had graced some of Cukor's early screen comedies) were much more at home in the farcical *Two-Faced Woman* than Garbo herself was.

The coup de grace was administered to this hapless motion picture by the National Legion of Decency, which rated the moral suitability of movies for its Catholic subscribers, as noted earlier in connection with *Her Cardboard Lover* (1942). *Two-Faced Woman* had already been filmed with Constance Talmadge in the pre-Legion days as *Her Sister from Paris* (1925). But at this point in history the Legion now took exception to the premise of the plot, according to which Karin Blake (Greta Garbo) temporarily masquerades as her fictitious twin sister "Katrin" in order to win back her erring husband, Larry (Melvyn Douglas), from his mistress of long standing, Gliselde Vaughan (Constance Bennett). Because of the adulterous implications of the storyline, the Legion classified *Two-Faced Woman* in its category of condemned films. To make matters worse, the Archbishop of New York, Francis Spellman, and several other clergymen across the land followed the Legion's lead and denounced the film as well.

Distressed that the Legion's widely publicized denunciation was earning the film an unjustified reputation with the public at large as a salacious movie, MGM panicked and temporarily withdrew the picture from distribution. The studio then inserted a brief scene into the film intended to imply that Karin's husband is wise to her scheme, thereby eradicating any possible hint of adulterous intent on his part in pursuing "Katrin."

But this additional footage only partially mollified the guardians of movie morality, since Larry's adulterous affair with Gliselde was still firmly entrenched in the plot. Hence the Legion only raised the rating of *Two-Faced Woman* from its condemned category to its still-disapproving objectionable category. In any event, it was far too late by this time to woo the mass audience to see the film anyway, given the poor notices that Garbo's performance received and the notoriety generated by the Legion's condemnation of the film. Asked about the furor created by the Legion's severe treatment of the film, Cukor replies that he considered the movie a lightweight comedy that was never intended to be taken so seriously. Whatever the film's flaws, when we see it today we discover the tasteful discretion so characteristic of Cukor's directorial style in handling slightly saucy subject matter. "I think vulgarity is the besetting sin of the picture business," he says; "but unfortunately you cannot legislate good taste. I wish you could."

Although *Two-Faced Woman* turned out to be Garbo's last movie, to say that the film destroyed her career is a vast oversimplification. For one thing, although the movie's disappointing reception made her more cautious in choosing her next subject, she had no thought of retiring from the screen for good at that time. For another, Garbo's pictures had always depended on the European market in order to turn a profit; and she finally decided to wait until the Second World War was over, when the overseas market would once again be open to her films, before making another film.

After the war Garbo chose for her comeback film an adaptation of *La Duchesse de Langeais,* a tired old melodrama which Cukor declined to direct. When the producers of the movie, to be shot in Rome, failed to live up to their contractual agreements with her, however, Cukor urged her to cancel her involvement in the project. "She has not attempted to make another movie since," Cukor notes; "but by dropping out of pictures when she did, Garbo has preserved her legendary screen image intact for all time."

Joan Crawford and *The Women* (1939)

During the same period in which Cukor made two Garbo films, he also directed three movies with Joan Crawford, another reigning queen of the Metro lot. The first of these, *The Women*, also included in its all-female cast several other top-flight actresses employed at MGM in those days, including Norma Shearer, Rosalind Russell, Paulette Goddard, Joan Fontaine, Ruth Hussey, and Marjorie Main. "*The Women* was a three-ring circus," says Cukor; and he was the ringmaster in charge of this superlative cluster of stars.

Cukor was assigned to direct *The Women* after Victor Fleming replaced him as director of *Gone With the Wind* (see Chapter 7); he was in turn replacing Ernst Lubitsch (who had taken over *One Hour with You* from Cukor back in 1932), so that Lubitsch could direct *Ninotchka*.

The Women was based on Claire Booth Luce's smash Broadway play about a group of wealthy New York socialites whose principal occupation seems to be exchanging gossip about each other. Their flighty existence is nicely keynoted in the opening scene in which Cukor's camera rapidly tours a beauty salon, allowing the viewer to catch snatches of the ladies' conversations. It finally comes to rest on Sylvia Fowler (Rosalind Russell) just as she hears the choice bit of gossip that sets the plot in motion. It seems that the husband of Mary Haines (Norma Shearer) is seeing Crystal Allen (Joan Crawford), a salesgirl at the perfume counter in a department store; and Mary's "friends" lose no time in spreading the news.

In casting the picture Cukor persuaded the front office at Joan Crawford's behest to choose her for the role of Crystal, which was considered by the studio to be a supporting part unworthy of a star of her stature. Cukor argued on Ms. Crawford's behalf that this small, meaty role was just right for her and that she would give a major performance that would be worthy of a star.

Cukor's support of Ms. Crawford's candidacy for the role of Crystal was more than vindicated in the scene in which Crystal chats over the phone with Mary Haines's husband, her lover of the moment: she purrs into the receiver, all cool calculation and bogus charm. "Her pseudo-uppercrust accent," Stephen Harvey observes, "is perfect; the emblem of a hardboiled tart trying to acquire some class in a hurry."[5]

Although Cukor admired Ms. Crawford's acting abilities, he found that occasionally she could be very trying to work with. Because of her longstanding professional rivalry with Norma Shearer at Metro, Ms. Crawford was not above finding ways during production to irritate Ms. Shearer. Cukor recalls Norma Shearer as a taut, nervous actress who, despite a veneer of serene self-confidence, "needed sympathy and reassurance," and who could therefore be easily flustered by Ms. Crawford's petty tricks.[6]

"Joan could behave in a very foolish way," he says, remembering that during one rehearsal Crawford sat on the sidelines knitting while she fed cues to Shearer. "Joan had these big knitting needles which she noisily clacked together," he says, just so she could needle Ms. Shearer into blowing her lines; but he put a stop to it. "Joan was just being an ass," Cukor concludes. "I liked Joan very much, except when she was acting in this idiotic fashion."

Besides securing the part of Crystal for Joan Crawford, Cukor also sold the studio on giving Joan Fontaine, who had yet to come into her own as an actress, the role of Peggy Day. Ms. Fontaine played the scene in which Peggy is reconciled with her estranged husband on the telephone with such force and feeling, says Cukor, that for the first time she realized that she was truly meant to be an actress. Recalling this experience years later, Ms. Fontaine paid Cukor this compliment: "I learned more about acting from one sentence of George Cukor's then from all my years of acting lessons." His advice was simply this: "Think and feel, and the rest will take care of itself."[7]

Among the other players, Rosalind Russell is at her madcap best as the daffy Sylvia Fowler, chief gossip in her tribe of friends. "The amazing thing is that she had never done a comedy part before," Cukor notes. "She had always played head nurses and secretaries. But in *The Women* she proved that she was the most darling, intelligent comedienne." In fact, in surveying her career, one critic has written that the difference between the Rosalind Russell of a movie like *The Women* and of a later vehicle like *Auntie Mame* (1958) is the difference between a comedienne and an institution.

The uniform excellence of the performances which Cukor elicited from all of the actresses in *The Women*, regardless of the relative size of their individual roles, vindicates the old adage that there are no minor roles, only minor performances. This is especially true of Joan Crawford's highly polished portrayal of the greedy gold digger Crystal, which remains a classic of its kind and stands out as one of the movie's principal assets. So does the film's visual inventiveness, which is obvious right from the start: during the opening credits each of the main characters is identified with a particular breed of animal. Mary Haines is pictured as a doe, Crystal Allen as a tigress, Sylvia Fowler as a cat, Peggy Day as a lamb, etc.

The one clear liability of the film is a fashion show which was interpolated at the insistence of the producer. Though the rest of the movie is in black and white, this sequence was shot in lush color, the better to show off the flashy clothes that were on display. Cukor

Hedda Hopper (in one of her famous hats), emerging comedienne Rosalind Russell, Norma Shearer and newcomer Joan Fontaine in the film version of Clare Boothe's The Women *(1939).*

objected that this sequence was supremely superfluous and slowed down the pace of the action, but to no avail. Current prints of the film present the fashion show in black and white, however, so that it stands out less like a sore thumb than it did in its original gaudy color version.

Despite this flaw in the film, *The Women* is by and large better and funnier on the screen than it was on the stage, thanks to the acid wit contributed to the screenplay by Anita Loos and Jane Murfin, who were principally responsible for the final shooting script—although seven other uncredited writers, including Donald Ogden Stewart and F. Scott Fitzgerald, had something to do with it along the way.

Little of the material that Scott Fitzgerald devised for the screenplay found its way into the final shooting script, but Cukor retained a personal admiration for the writer that dated back to his directing the stage version of Fitzgerald's *Great Gatsby* on Broadway in 1926. Besides *The Women*, Fitzgerald had also worked on the screenplay of *Gone With the Wind* during the period in which Cukor was associated with the production, and Cukor accordingly invited

Fitzgerald to lunch one day for old time's sake. "Yet it seemed we had nothing to talk about," Cukor remembers. "Fitzgerald looked grim and ate in silence. I told him that the only people I had ever known to eat as fast as he did had both died young." A year or so later, so did Fitzgerald.

The Women was remade in color in 1956 as a musical under the title *The Opposite Sex*. Despite David Miller's competent direction and a serviceable cast headed by veterans like June Allyson and Joan Blondell, the remake lacks the panache and verve of Cukor's tough, affectionate treatment of the same story. Like *High Society*, the musical remake of *The Philadelphia Story*, *The Opposite Sex* has consequently not superseded Cukor's stylish original.

Susan and God (1940)

When *The Women* went into release in the fall of 1939, Cukor then set to work on the film adaptation of *Susan and God* (1940). Based on the 1937 Rachel Crothers stage success, the plot centers on flightly, self-deluded Susan Trexel, who nearly drives her family and friends mad when she temporarily experiences a phony religious conversion. The title is derived from *Romeo and Juliet*, in which Juliet's nurse says of her deceased daughter, "Susan is with God; She was too good for me" (Act I, scene iii, lines 20–21). Susan Trexel thinks she is too good for her family and friends; but she is, of course, quite wrong.

MGM had purchased the rights to the play with Norma Shearer in mind, but Shearer reluctantly turned down the part because she balked at playing the mother of a teenage daughter, fearing that she would be typed for middle-aged roles from then on. After considering Greer Garson for the role, Cukor then suggested that Joan Crawford play Susan. Crawford accepted the part because it was a juicy one, and she was bothered not in the slightest by playing a woman somewhat older than herself. "I'd play Wallace Beery's grandmother if it was a good part," she shrugged.

Unfortunately, although the script is by Anita Loos, one of the principal architects of the screenplay for *The Women*, the film is not in a class with the earlier picture. In spite of the fact that Ms. Loos created some fresh and funny scenes of her own for the film adaptation of *Susan and God*, the movie is static and stagebound in a way that Cukor's many other stage-derived films are not. As one critic complained, Cukor too often seems to group his actors around the settee in Susan's living room and just lets them talk.

Nonetheless, at other times he endeavors to make the movie come alive visually by his characteristically creative camera work. As Susan stands on the railway station platform awaiting the train that will take her away from her family to an evangelical congress, Cukor photographs her from across the railroad tracks. When the train arrives, therefore, it momentarily blocks the viewer's vision of Susan because it is standing between her and the camera. After it pulls out, Susan is revealed still standing on the platform preparing to return home. This visual surprise (used by many other movie directors since) neatly telegraphs to the filmgoer that Susan at last realizes that her witless neglect of her husband, Barry (Fredric March), and her daughter is not the way to serve God.

Cukor in principle has always avoided showy camera angles in his films because he agrees with Alfred Hitchcock that really good cinematography never draws attention to itself. Thus Hitchcock has said that he would never take a shot from behind the flames in a fireplace with the camera looking outward toward the room, presumably photographing the action through the blaze, because in real life it would be humanly impossible for anyone to observe the scene from such an incredible angle. But Cukor has just such a shot in one of the living-room scenes in *Susan and God,* in which the camera records the action at one point apparently from inside the fireplace. One cannot blame Cukor for trying to instill some visual variety into this essentially talky scene, something which, as I have said, the movie as a whole could have used more of; but the fact remains that the pretentious camera angle from which this shot is photographed does distract the filmgoer from the dialogue of the scene. Otherwise Cukor's camera work in the movie is as unobtrusive as ever.

Cukor was pleased with Crawford's portrayal of Susan, and indeed her performance is a definite plus in an otherwise rather routine film. "Playing a flibbertigibbet like Susan was a real change of pace for Joan," he notes; "and I think she was awfully good." He therefore looked forward to directing her in what would surely be one of the most demanding roles she was ever likely to play.

A Woman's Face (1941)

It was Joan Crawford's own idea to film *A Woman's Face,* a remake of a Swedish film called *En kvinnas ansikte,* in which Ingrid Bergman had starred in her native land before Selznick imported her to Hollywood. The screenplay was mostly the work of Donald Ogden

Stewart, Cukor's frequent collaborator, who looked at the earlier movie and then concocted his own version of the story. The murder trial of Anna Holm (Joan Crawford) provides the narrative framework for the series of flashbacks which detail Anna's sordid past. It seems that Anna's face was severely burned in childhood, causing her to grow up to be a bitter, alienated woman, disfigured in body and soul.

As if to take revenge on the world for her affliction, Anna then fell into a life of crime, and the first flashback shows her operating an inn situated deep in a dark forest, which serves as a front for her criminal activities. The decadent atmosphere of this disreputable place is established by, among other things, a glimpse of two Lesbians dancing together. Anna first appears as a spectral figure enveloped in shadows, symbolic of her murky, morose state of soul. Then she steps into the light which piteously exposes her hideously marred features. It is a stunning moment.

Anna's physical scar is eventually removed by Dr. Segert, a plastic surgeon (Melvyn Douglas), but the festering psychic wounds that have resulted from years of facial disfigurement continue to persist, largely unhealed. (Since Anna's looks are restored in the course of the movie, this picture could have been more appropriately entitled *Two-Faced Woman* than the Garbo movie of that title which Cukor directed immediately afterward.)

In league with the satanic Torsten Barring (Conrad Veidt) Anna plots the murder of Barring's young nephew Lars Erik, whose death will bring Barring a large inheritance which he and Anna hope to share. After becoming the lad's governess, Anna plans to murder him while they are passing over a waterfall in a cable car and the boy is absorbed in the view.

Cukor squeezes every ounce of suspense out of the scene aboard the cable car by employing close shots of Anna's hand surreptitiously inching toward the safety latch that she means to release in order to send the unsuspecting youngster hurtling to his death in the raging waters below; these shots are deftly intercut with close-ups of Anna's pained expression, which mirrors the crisis of conscience she is experiencing at the last moment.

In the end Anna not only spares the boy's life, but later shoots Barring just as he is about to murder Lars Erik himself. At film's end Anna is acquitted of the murder charge brought against her for killing her late accomplice; and she walks out of the courtroom on the arm of Dr. Segert, the benign physician who serves as an instrument of both physical and spiritual healing for Anna in the course of the movie.

(Segert observes at one point that he has brought Anna to life the way that Pygmalion did Galatea in classical mythology, thus presaging Cukor's *My Fair Lady* [1964], based on Shaw's play *Pygmalion*.)

Carlos Clarens is quite correct when he writes that Barring and Segert together epitomize the moral conflict that rages within Anna throughout the picture. Her relationship with the compassionate doctor gradually inspires her to decent and humane behavior, and ultimately counteracts entirely the brutalizing influence which her iniquitous coconspirator exercised over her for so long. Joan Crawford depicts Anna's gradual change of heart superbly, and in so doing gives under Cukor's direction what is perhaps the greatest performance of her career, just as Garbo has done in *Camille*.

Ms. Crawford recalls in her autobiography that Cukor was concerned that she might overplay the big courtroom scene in which Anna recounts the details of her wretched childhood, culminating in the tragic accident that left her scarred for so many years. Ms. Crawford says that, in order to insure that she did not overact in this particular scene, Cukor rehearsed the very life out of her. Then, just

Joan Crawford in A Woman's Face *(1941), the most demanding part of her whole career.*

before the cameras turned, "Mr. Cukor had me recite the multiplication table by twos until all emotion was drained and I was totally exhausted, my voice dwindled to a tired monotone." At that point Cukor said, "Now Anna, tell us the story of your life," and proceeded to shoot the scene.[9] Needless to say, Ms. Crawford gave a beautifully understated reading of the scene.

Cukor was more than satisfied with Ms. Crawford's performance in *A Woman's Face*. "It was the first time that Joan played, and uncompromisingly so, a bitch of a woman; and she was excellent," he comments. "I feel she should have won an Academy Award for *A Woman's Face*, as she did a few years later for *Mildred Pierce* (1945)." In point of fact, Cukor has always felt that her Oscar for *Mildred Pierce* implicitly represented a sort of delayed recognition on the part of the film industry of Ms. Crawford's work in earlier films like *A Woman's Face*.

Judy Holliday and *Born Yesterday* (1950)

If Cukor's creative association with Joan Crawford came at a time when she was an established star, his professional alliance with Judy Holliday commenced at the beginning of her career, as had also been the case with Cukor and Katharine Hepburn. Ms. Holliday's role in her first Cukor picture, *Winged Victory* (1944), had admittedly been a minor one. When she returned to the screen after making her mark on Broadway in Garson Kanin's play *Born Yesterday,* however, Cukor cast her in a much more substantial role in *Adam's Rib* (1949). She then went on to star in three Cukor films, the first of which was the screen version of *Born Yesterday* (1950).

Cukor was scheduled to direct *Born Yesterday* at Columbia and wanted very much to have the young actress recreate her original stage role in the film. But Harry Cohn, who was in charge of production at Columbia, preferred Rita Hayworth to Judy Holliday, since Cohn thought Ms. Holliday simply lacked the star quality that the glamorous Ms. Hayworth possessed.

As a result, Cukor, Tracy and Hepburn, and Ruth Gordon and Garson Kanin became secret partners in a conspiracy to showcase Judy Holliday's performance in *Adam's Rib* in a manner that would convince Cohn that she was quite capable of assuming the starring role in *Born Yesterday*. With Cukor's approval, the Kanins built up Ms. Holliday's part in the screenplay of *Adam's Rib* and Katharine Hepburn allowed the younger actress to dominate more than one of their scenes together, particularly the one in which Ms. Hepburn interviewed Ms. Holliday in jail, as noted above. In the wake of all this behind-the-scenes plotting by Cukor and his cohorts during the production of *Adam's Rib*, Judy Holliday won the female lead in *Born Yesterday* and an Oscar in the bargain.

As Billie Dawn, Ms. Holliday rendered an archetypical portrait of a beautiful but dumb blonde. An ex-chorine, Billie is the mistress of a wealthy junk dealer, Harry Brock (Broderick Crawford), who is determined to buy his way into Washington power politics. Harry engages Paul Verrall (William Holden) to give the scantily educated Billie an elementary course in political science, so that she will not embarrass him when he is entertaining the politicians he hopes to bribe.

Proving that she was not born yesterday after all, Billie learns enough from Paul to know that what Harry is doing is vile; and she threatens to expose his plans unless he abandons them (a situation which closely parallels the way what Kitty Packard handles her husband in *Dinner at Eight* [1933] when she learns about his unsavory business deals). As one critic drolly sums up *Born Yesterday,* Billie's behavior is an illustration of the old maxim that if you lead a whore to culture you can make her think.

The first draft of the script for the film was done by Albert Mannheimer, who presumably worked on the assumption that a screenwriter is not exercising his own creativity unless he makes significant alterations in the work that he is adapting for the screen. Cukor recalls taking one look at this version of the screenplay and turning it down flat, since the writer had jettisoned some excellent material in Kanin's play. "And then Garson Kanin, not paid for it, did the work," says Cukor; "and we got it back to what it was."[10]

Kanin, who received no screen credit as well as no fee for composing the final shooting script for *Born Yesterday,* did more than simply restore the goodies that Mannheimer had excised from the play. Taking his cue from references in the original dialogue to several Washington landmarks that Billie mentions visiting, he opened out the play by constructing several scenes that were filmed on locations at these very sites.

"We shot scenes at places like the Jefferson Memorial and the Capitol," says Cukor; "and this gave the picture greater mobility." These scenes also served to dramatize more vividly than was feasible within the confines of the stage the way in which Billie's systematic tour of the city's historic monuments enables her for the very first time in her life to discover for herself America's rich and meaningful past, and consequently to see Harry's crass attempts to manipulate elected government officials for his own aggrandizement as a perversion of the democratic principles on which this country was founded.

The key interior set in the film was Harry's huge Washington hotel suite, and Cukor's camera explored virtually every inch of this elaborate set as he moved the action from room to room to keep the film from turning into a mere photographed stage play. Conversely, Cukor had no qualms about shooting the famous gin-rummy game sequence with a stationary camera from a single angle, in acknowledgment of Ms. Holliday's power to hold the moviegoer's attention as Billie repeatedly bested Harry in hand after hand. "The quiet, blank-faced assurance of the girl," writes Gordon Gow, "and the riffling of the cards in her deliberate hands reduced her opponent to a jelly of nervous frustration."[11] Commenting on this scene, Cukor explains, "My rule of thumb is this: unless moving the camera is going to contribute something to the scene in question, let it remain at rest."

Throughout the movie Judy Holliday demonstrates her ability to make us laugh at Billie's dim-witted remarks, at the very same time that she is stirring our compassion for Billie's vulnerable stupidity. In one scene the apelike Harry becomes so exasperated with Billie that he strikes her savagely across the face. As she whimpers and cries softly, we realize just how deeply the actress has made us care for Billie. Cukor admired this knack of Ms. Holliday's for touching a moviegoer's heart as well as his funny bone. "It is a rare quality, possessed by only the truely great comediennes," he notes. "And Judy had it to a superlative degree."

The Marrying Kind (1952)

In *The Marrying Kind* Cukor once again drew on Judy Holliday's ability to create a character who was at once both humorous and sympathetic, this time in the role of Florence Keefer, who is bent on divorcing her husband, Chet (Aldo Ray). Like *Adam's Rib*, this original screenplay was written by Ruth Gordon and Garson Kanin and is therefore characterized by their finely honed dialogue. When, for example, the understanding divorce judge, Anna Carroll (played by silent screen star Madge Kennedy), asks Florence and Chet the reason for their incompatability, Florence answers without hesita-

Broderick Crawford and Judy Holliday in the legendary gin rummy game in Born Yesterday *(1950), the film for which she won an Academy Award.*

tion, "Because we're married to each other." Later Chet is embarrassed to admit to Judge Carroll in front of Florence that he once loved his estranged wife very much, and so he dodges the question with this touching reply: "She told me I did; and she was right."

The underlying problem with their marriage which Florence and Chet find it hard to grasp is that both of them harbored unrealistic expectations of each other; and this fact progressively becomes clearer in the flashbacks in which each of them tells about their life together. Often we hear the voice of one of them narrating a past incident on the sound track while we simultaneously see the same episode acted out before us on the screen as it is remembered quite differently by the other party. As the judge points out to them, "It's all in what you remember and in your point of view."

Their romantic illusions about their marriage are finally shattered completely by the tragic death of their small son Joey during a Fourth of July picnic. Judge Carroll suggests to them that this crushing crisis, which initially had driven them apart, can now be the source of their reconciliation as they seek to give some emotional support to each other. In this way Florence and Chet will hopefully be able to confirm their original conviction that both of them still are the marrying kind, and hence should stay wedded to each other.

Cukor sought to create the couple's lower-middle-class milieu in the film as authentically as possible, both by extensive location shooting in and around New York City and by the realistic detail of the studio sets, like the Keefers' narrow, cluttered flat. Their apartment comes to symbolize the stifling sense of confinement which Florence and Chet begin to feel, once the tensions between them start to close in on them and the bonds of matrimony turn to chains, yoking them together in mutual captivity.

In contrast to the unmitigated realism of most of the movie, there is a dream sequence which occurs midway through the picture. All three of the original screenplays which Ruth Gordon and Garson Kanin coauthored for Cukor, including *Adam's Rib* (1949) and *Pat and Mike* (1952), contain such a fantasy sequence; but the best one is in *The Marrying Kind*. Chet, who is a post-office employee, has a nightmare in which he is sucked downward off the bed on which he is sleeping onto a conveyer belt which transports him to a mail shute, down which he slides as if her were a parcel into the nether regions of the post office where he works. Clad only in his underwear, he surfaces in Times Square, where a firing squad composed of multiple images of Florence dressed in a policeman's uniform shoots him dead, thereby recalling his favorite retort to his nagging wife's complaints about him, "Shoot me at sunrise!"

This fantasy sequence brilliantly visualizes Chet's subconscious anxiety that he is being slowly dehumanized by his monotonous, frustrating job at the post office, where he feels that he is treated no better than the packages which he processes, and that he is being unmanned by his strong-willed wife, who is pictured in Chet's dream wearing male attire—something which he, caught without his trousers, obviously lacks.

The most crucial episode in the movie, however, is the flashback to the holiday picnic at which Joey dies. The camera does not follow the boy as he darts off to the nearby lake for a swim, but holds on Florence as she merrily plunks her ukulele and warbles a chorus or two of "Dolores." In the background behind her the moviegoer sees the legs of several picnickers running toward the lake in obvious haste. But Florence is oblivious to the mounting crisis, until her little girl rushes up to her shouting that Joey has drowned. Florence becomes hysterical, and the sequence ends with a dissolve from Florence sobbing inconsolably over Joey's body to her breaking down all over again as she relives this wrenching catastrophe for Judge Carroll.

While it is true that Judy Holliday is remarkably good in sequences like the one just described, it would be unfair to slight Aldo Ray's sensitive and compelling performance in the movie. Although Sid Caesar had initially been considered for the part, Cukor was so impressed with the disarmingly natural style of acting which Ray had exhibited in his test for the part that Cukor finally gave the role of Chet to him. Once shooting began, however, Ray froze in front of the camera just as Shelley Winters had done when she began work on *A Double Life* (1947). With the reassurances of both his director and his costar, Ray settled in to his part after a day or two, and gave the performance of his life.

The Marrying Kind recalls *Sylvia Scarlett* (1936) in that it begins as pure comedy and moves closer to serious drama as the romantic notions of the main characters are stripped away. It was perhaps somewhat risky for him to blend comedy and drama as he did in these two films, Cukor concedes; "but, after all, isn't that how things sometimes happen in life?"

It Should Happen to You (1954)

The Marrying Kind also has an affinity with *It Should Happen to You* because in it Judy Holliday is once again cast as a heroine who, like many other of Cukor's central characters, must give up her unrealistic expectations of what life holds in store for her if she is to find genuine personal happiness. *It Should Happen to You* was penned by Garson Kanin, who wrote or cowrote all of the Cukor films in which Judy Holliday played, from *Adam's Rib* onward. This time around she plays an obtuse blonde reminiscent of Billie Dawn who is named Gladys Glover (Kanin borrowed the name from a young girl mentioned in his wife's screenplay for *The Actress* [1953] who in fact never appears in that film.)

In *It Should Happen to You* Gladys Glover is an ordinary New York working girl who suffers an identity crisis when she loses her job. Determined to make a name for herself in the world at large one way or another, this goofy young lady spends her last cent to rent a gigantic billboard in Columbus Circle just to put her name before the public. The explorer after whom Columbus Circle is named may have discovered America, but Gladys Glover wants America to discover her! (Given the plot of the picture, one wonders why the original title of the film, *A Name for Herself*, was not retained.)

Almost instantly Gladys achieves a kind of freakish notoriety, but her boyfriend Pete Sheppard (Jack Lemmon) persuades her that fame which is not founded on some sort of personal achievement which merits renown is empty and meaningless. Gladys accordingly renounces her spurious celebrity status and happily allows Pete to shepherd her back into obscurity by making her Mrs. Pete Sheppard.

It Should Happen to You marked the screen debut of Jack Lemmon, who came to films after briefly working in television. Unseasoned film actor that he was, Lemmon tended to overact during the first week or so of shooting. Whenever this happened, Cukor would get Lemmon to tone down his performance by reminding him that the first rule of thumb for a film actor is that "less is more." After listening to Cukor tell him this several times, Lemmon finally became furious and demanded to know if the director was trying to tell him *not* to act. "Oh, God, yes!" was Cukor's reply. Today Lemmon says that he has never forgotten that experience. "I've learned my craft from that advice," he says. "It's the hardest thing in the world to be simple, and the easiest thing in the world to act your brains out and make an ass of yourself.">[12] Like Joan Fontaine, Angela Lansbury, and others before him, Lemmon got advice from Cukor early in his career that served him in good stead ever after.

That Cukor managed to elicit a fairly relaxed performance from Lemmon is exemplified in the bar scene, in which Pete and Gladys engage in a little impromptu harmonizing on the old Harold Arlen standard "Let's Fall in Love." "Pete and Gladys were supposedly just casually playing around at the piano, singing and chatting," Cukor remembers; and the scene developed so naturally that more than one critic assumed the action was entirely improvised right on the spot while the cameras were rolling. "Actually we carefully rehearsed the whole thing over and over again to make it look spontaneous and unrehearsed," Cukor explains. "As I have often said, I depend on rehearsal rather than on improvisation to make a scene work; and this principle, as I have mentioned in connection with my films with Garbo, was her rule too."

This is not to say that Cukor does not make room for the inspiration of the moment when he is rehearsing a scene. While working out a quarrel scene with Lemmon and Holliday, Cukor had the uneasy feeling that it was not really very believable. Suddenly the director asked Lemmon how he usually reacted when he was genuinely angry. "I always get cramps in the stomach," the actor responded. Cukor told him to add that bit of business to the action; and so, in the next take Lemmon doubled over as if he were suffering from pains in his stomach. The addition of that one detail made the entire scene more true to life, Cukor concludes, "because it gave the action the texture of reality."

Among the film's fringe benefits is a hilarious take-off on TV talk shows in which Gladys participates on a panel with, among others, Constance Bennett, a frequent Cukor star of the 1930s. Gladys stops the show with this candid comment on teenage sexual mores: "If they're big enough, they're old enough!" It is in such scenes that Judy Holliday proves what a gifted comedienne she really was. "Judy was only in her forties when she died," says Cukor. "It is a pity that she was still so young at the time of her death, because she could have gone on doing wonderful things in pictures." *It Should Happen to You* was the last Cukor film in which Ms. Holliday appeared. Though she went on to make other movies before her untimely death, like Garbo and Crawford and others before her, Judy Holliday was never better than when she was being directed by George Cukor.

Lana Turner and A *Life of Her Own* (1950)

Like *It Should Happen to You, A Life of Her Own* is another study
of a young woman obsessed with gaining fame, this time in the world
of high fashion. It starred, appropriately enough, one of the most
glamorous actresses of the period, Lana Turner. Nevertheless, Cukor
did not want to direct the film because he thought the plotline weak.
"But I was not committed to directing a picture at the moment; and
since I was under contract to MGM, I was getting paid for not
working. So I was taken in irons to the office of Dore Schary, a top
studio executive, for a conference about this movie. As he outlined
the scenario for me, I kept saying to myself about one hackneyed plot
contrivance or another, 'Oh, my God, they're not going to use *that*
old chestnut again!'" (The heroine's sending her lover back to his
invalid wife recalls Zaza's equally soap-operatic renunciation of her
married lover, for example.) "I resisted Schary's effort to get me to
take the assignment; but since I owed the studio a picture, in the end
I could not in conscience turn it down. So I paid my debt to society
and made the film. But it was the last picture I ever directed that I did
not personally want to make."

The script was the work of Isobel Lennart (*Funny Girl*), Cukor
continues; "and although I thought the story basically silly and fatu-
ous, a few of the scenes that she had written were fascinating." Some
of the film's best sequences center on Mary Ashlon (Ann Dvorak), an
aging model who succumbs to drink and drugs, and finally takes her
own life.

Lily James (Lana Turner) fails to profit from Mary's pathetic example; and by the end of the movie she has experienced a professional
decline and fall similar to Mary's. It is painfully obvious to Lily by
then that she has failed to forge for herself a successful life of her own,
as she had planned to do when she first arrived in New York City, a
fresh-faced, intrepid young lady with a promising modeling career
before her. Hence, at the fade-out, as she wanders aimlessly in the
night through the dark city streets, it is very likely that Lily will
inevitably continue to follow Mary's downward path to despair until
she too kills herself, especially since she smashes on the pavement
the figurine which Mary had given her as a good luck charm just
before she walks off into the darkness.

In actual fact the original ending of the film left no doubt whatever
about Lily's ultimate fate, but the scene depicting her suicide was
part of the substantial amount of footage that was excised from the

movie before it went into general release after its premiere engagements. "The picture was chopped to ribbons," says Cukor stoically.
The studio reduced the movie's running time from 150 to 108 minutes, presumably in a futile attempt to make the film seem less
pessimistic and therefore more palatable to the taste of the general
public. Since *A Life of Her Own* shares the same somber vision and
dark ambience of Cukor's other exercises in *film noir* such as *Keeper
of the Flame* (1943) and *A Double Life* (1947), however, no amount of
tampering with the finished product could make the pervasive tone
and texture of the movie seem any less bleak.

Ava Gardner and *Bhowani Junction* (1956)

Bhowani Junction was also recut to some extent by the studio after
Cukor finished it, though not nearly so drastically as *A Life of Her
Own*. The action of this film, based on John Masters's best-selling
novel, is set at the time of the British withdrawal from India in 1947,
and is concerned with a nurse in the British army named Victoria
Jones, an Anglo-Indian girl (Ava Gardner), who becomes amorously
involved with no less than three different men in the course of the
film: Col. Savage, a British officer (Stewart Granger), Ranjit Kasel, an
Indian (Francis Matthews), and Patrick Taylor, an Anglo-Indian like
herself (Bill Travers). The diverse ethnic backgrounds of Victoria's
three lovers are meant to mirror how Victoria, as a girl who is
half-English and half-Indian, finds her personal life affected by the
clash of cultures that has existed in India as long as the country has
been under British rule. The resultant split in her own personality is
crystallized by her often wearing a wispy Indian sari wrapped around
her smart English skirt and blouse.

When the film was previewed, however, some members of the
audience seemed to be unsympathetic to the heroine, seeing her as
some sort of slut being passed from man to man. The front office at
MGM consequently decreed that the film must undergo some alterations before it was released in order to put Victoria in a more favorable
light. A narrative frame was accordingly added to the story in which
Col. Savage explains to a brother officer aboard a train precisely how
Victoria's status as a half-caste caused her to become embroiled in the
smouldering racial and political tensions of the time.

Savage begins telling Victoria's story to his traveling companion as
they start out on their journey, continues to comment on the action,
voice-over on the sound track, as her history unfolds in a series of

Ava Gardner and Bill Travers emoting in Cukor's "Eastern," Bhowani Junction, *set in India (1956).*

flashbacks, and then wraps up the tale at the end of the movie as the train reaches its destination. In the last analysis this narrative frame is really of little consequence, since a moviegoer either relates with compassion to Victoria's plight—in which case the commentary is superfluous—or he does not—in which case the commentary is futile, because the most elaborate explanation of her behavior will not suffice to move the moviegoer to identify sympathetically with Victoria if he does not feel so inclined.

Besides, if one pays attention as the film unreels, it is sufficiently clear—quite apart from Savage's voice-over commentary—that each of Victoria's three lovers implicitly represents a different cultural option for her. She first rejects Taylor because he has not come to terms with being a halfbreed any better than she has; she later breaks her engagement to her aristocratic Indian fiancé because, try as she might, she will never be able to acclimate herself to his old-world customs and attitudes; and she finally accepts the British colonel's marriage proposal, but only on the condition that they continue to live in India, since she knows that she would never feel at home in

England. "I belong here," Victoria explains to Savage, "not as a phony Indian or as a phony white, but as myself." In this way does Victoria solve both her cultural and romantic conflicts at one and the same time.

Over and above the tinkering with *Bhowani Junction* ordered by the studio, the industry censors insisted on what Cukor calls some prudish cuts in the picture. The censorship board deleted a love scene in which Patrick Taylor disappears below the frame while the camera remains on Victoria's ecstatic countenance, even though Cukor has thus discreetly implied cunnilingus in this scene by artistic indirection, and not portrayed it explicitly.

Another censorship cut in the film, which appears to be even more arbitrary than the one just mentioned, occurs in the scene in which Victoria temporarily shares Savage's quarters aboard a military train. The censors excised a shot in which Victoria dips Savage's toothbrush in a glass of scotch and cleans her teeth with his brush. Her use of Savage's brush is admittedly a sign of intimacy between the pair, but if the guardians of the motion picture code removed this shot because they thought that Victoria's putting Savage's toothbrush in her mouth implied some sort of symbolic fellatio, as one suspects that they did, their thinking in this instance was very far-fetched indeed.

In spite of the alterations made in the film by both the studio and the censor board, *Bhowani Junction* still stands as proof positive that the ravishing Ava Gardner was an excellent actress as well as a sultry beauty. Under Cukor's direction she met the demands of her exacting role quite adequately, although Cukor admits to "cheating a little" to make her performance in a quarrel scene better still.

As Cukor tells the story, it seems that Ms. Gardner had lunched with a Hollywood reporter just prior to shooting the scene in question, and had returned to the set furious because of the prying questions which had been put to her by the journalist about her personal life. While Cukor was coaching the actress for the upcoming scene, he said, "Get mad, the way that you did this afternoon with that rude gossip columnist." Just as Ms. Gardner's face flushed with renewed rage, Cukor started to shoot the scene. After the take was over, Ms. Gardner realized that the director had deliberately gotten her agitated by mentioning her unpleasant luncheon encounter and exclaimed with feigned irritation, "You son-of-a-bitch, I'll never tell you anything that happens to me off the set again, because somehow you will find a way of using it in the film!" Cukor replied serenely, "I'm not above taking advantage of anger or anything else that will improve a scene."

Cukor was less satisfied with the studio's selection of Stewart Granger to play the gruff, aging Col. Savage than he was with the choice of Gardner for the role of Victoria. He would have preferred an older actor like Trevor Howard, since Granger was more of a handsome movie star than a dramatic actor. Howard, Cukor feels, would have given a much more forceful performance that Granger did; and the whole movie would have been the better for it.

The location work for the film was done in Lahore, Pakistan, where the film unit was offered more cooperation than the government of India was willing to extend. In Pakistan, Cukor and company were supplied with the services of troops from the Thirteenth Battalion Frontier Force and trains from the Northern Railway for use in the movie's more spectacular sequences.

Because the personal story of Victoria Jones is set against a panoramic background of apocalyptic political and social upheavals, Cukor was able to employ the wide screen to great advantage in staging the assortment of riots, train wrecks, and other large-scale episodes that mark *Bhowani Junction* as one of the most ambitious epics of Cukor's career in pictures. In directing these king-sized sequences, Cukor demonstrates his ability to "personalize" a crowd scene by focusing on individuals within the group. Like Cecil B. DeMille, Cukor is very much aware that audiences cannot easily identify with an anonymous mob of people, but only with individuals who are participants in and representatives of the larger group.

Working in close collaboration with the brilliant cinematographer Freddie Young (*Lawrence of Arabia*), Cukor employs this sound directorial principle very effectively in the scene in which a train is sabotaged by a group of rabidly anti-British insurgents bent on hastening the departure of the British from their country. As Victoria ministers to the suffering casualties lying in the wreckage, Cukor captures their individual torment by punctuating long shots of mass hysteria and anguish with close shots of individual victims of the explosion. The overall atmosphere of the scene may be chaotic, but Cukor's handling of it decidedly is not.

Cukor of course does not slight drama for spectacle. One of the most powerful scenes in the film, in fact, involves only two characters. In it a seedy, sweaty British officer attempts to rape Victoria in a railroad yard, just as a train roars by. Like the relentless clamor of the passing elevated train that accompanies the murder in *A Double Life* (1947), Cukor's utilization of the unnerving screech of the strident train whistle to underscore the violence of the attempted rape in the present scene in *Bhowani Junction* is more effective in helping to overwhelm the audience with the brutal power of the scene than background music would have been.

Another strong dramatic sequence in the film focuses on the betrothal of Victoria and Ranjit in an Indian temple. As she kneels next to him during the ceremony, the liturgical prayers uttered by the ministers of the rite fade away on the sound track and are replaced by a chorus of warnings from a cross-section of people associated with Victoria's life, ranging from her English father to Ranjit's Indian mother. Their misgivings about the momentous step which she is taking are in reality an expression of Victoria's own ambivalence about her marriage to Ranjit. As their voices swell to a crescendo, she suddenly rises and flees the temple, unable to commit herself once and for all to an exclusively Indian life-style.

Although the Indian town of the title may be called a junction, it is evident in the film right up to the end that East remains East and West remains West, and these twain can only be made to meet in a genuine junction of mutual understanding as the result of a great deal of painful soul-searching, like that experienced by the Anglo-Indian Victoria Jones, in whose heart is distilled the cultural conflict which the film attempts to examine.

Anna Magnani and *Wild Is the Wind* (1957)

Besides directing home-grown actresses like Ava Gardner, Judy Holliday, and Joan Crawford, Cukor has also directed great ladies of the screen from other countries like the Swedish Garbo and two of Italy's finest, Anna Magnani and Sophia Loren. Cukor worked with Magnani on a picture called *Wild Is the Wind*.

The project came into being when Paramount bought the rights to *Furia*, a 1946 Italian film directed by Goffredo Alessandrini, in order to remake it as *Wild Is the Wind*, and hired John Sturges to direct. He decided instead to replace Fred Zinnemann as director of *The Old Man and the Sea* at Warners, after Zinnemann walked off that picture because of disagreements about location shooting conditions.

Cukor then took over *Wild Is the Wind*, a turbulent story of a rancher named Gino (Anthony Quinn) who imports his deceased wife's sister Gioia (Anna Magnani) from Italy to be his second bride. Gioia comes from a remote village in the Italian provinces, and she is baffled at every turn by the gadgets and gimmickry that distinguish a modern mechanized society like the United States. Only moments after landing at the airport, she is unable to cope with the intricacies of a mechanical coffee dispenser, which Gino has to operate for her.

Her initial uneasiness about living in unfamiliar surroundings is compounded by the constant references that Gino makes to his adored first wife, and his habit of absentmindedly calling Gioia by her dead sister's name, Rosanna. Cukor's frequent theme of illusion versus reality is illustrated in Gino's refusal to face the incontrovertible fact that the past is dead and buried, and that he must therefore relinquish his attempts to revive it. Specifically, he must give up his cherished fantasy of reliving his marriage to the mild-mannered, passive Rosanna by trying to retool his aggressive, irrepressible second wife into a replica of his first.

But the insensitive Gino fails to grasp this fact, despite Gioia's repeated endeavors to impress it upon him; and the resulting failure of communication that comes to exist between them is dramatized in a variety of ways. It is ironic, for example, that Gioia must learn English from records in order to bridge the language gap between herself and her American neighbors, when they often understand and sympathize with her better than Gino, who can converse fluently with his wife in her native tongue. Gino and Gioia may both speak Italian; but they simply are not able to conduct a dialogue on a deeper, more meaningful level.

By the same token, Gioia has a great affection for the wild stallion that she keeps on the ranch because, as she remarks pointedly to Gino, "This horse and I speak the same language." Clearly she and Gino do not. Both Gioia and the stallion, one infers, are by nature free spirits, creatures as wild as the wind who resist Gino's efforts to corral and tame them.

But the uncomprehending Gino can always be counted upon to miss the point; and so he has his ranch hands break the horse so that he can present it to Gioia as a birthday present. To Gino's surprise but no one else's, she is shocked and grieved when she beholds the once-proud animal wearing blinders and humbly pulling a carriage daintily festooned with flowers. Gioia rejects the gift, muttering disconsolately, "It was a horse before; now it's a sheep."

Resolving anew that Gino is not going to break her spirit in a similar manner, Gioia packs her grip to return to Italy. Gino intercepts her at the airport, however, and persuades her to give him another chance to learn to accept her for herself and not as a mere stand-in for her dead sister. Interestingly enough, Gioia successfully operates the coffee vending machine in the airport lounge this time, without any help from her husband. This circumstance implies that she is willing to accommodate herself to American ways and will continue to do so, if her husband will but have the consideration to make some adjustments on her behalf.

Cukor extracted a powerful, passionate performance from Ms. Magnani in this, her second American film, made after she won an Oscar for her first Hollywood picture, Tennessee Williams's *The Rose Tattoo* (1955). "Magnani was a tough type, brought up in the streets of Rome," says Cukor. "She was also a wonderful talent," a tempestuous actress who was able to radiate strong emotion on the screen as few other movie actresses could. She could also be extremely temperamental and difficult to work with, in contrast to Sophia Loren, whom Cukor remembers as "very human and modest, and easy to work with." He enjoyed directing Sophia Loren in *Heller in Pink Tights* (1960), which by coincidence also starred Anthony Quinn, Anna Magnani's costar from *Wild Is the Wind*.

Sophia Loren and *Heller in Pink Tights* (1960)

Heller in Pink Tights, Cukor's only Western, was based on a novel by Louis L'Amour, a native of South Dakota whose stories of the American frontier are generally considered to be not mere pulp fiction about the Old West, but well-researched historical novels. Thus Angela Rossini, the title character of *Heller in Pink Tights,* was inspired by the life of Adah Menken, whom the printed prologue of the movie informs us was a beautiful and flirtatious actress who swept through the Wild West with a theatrical troupe in pioneer days, and who was the toast of every settlement and tank town from Cheyenne to Virginia City. "What interested me about her and her troupe," Cukor explains, "was that in bringing culture to these frontier towns they were to that extent the torch bearers of civilization in the wilderness."

Because the company performs a number of historical plays, the costumes which the actors wear in the various productions in their repertory represent a variety of historical periods. George Hoynigen-Huene, the eminent fashion photographer who acted as color consultant on all of Cukor's color films from *A Star Is Born* (1954) through *The Chapman Report* (1962), therefore ransacked the Paramount wardrobe storage vaults and came up with a medley of costumes ranging from Roman togas to Renaissance tunics for the

traveling thespians to wear on stage in their endless barnstorming tours.

All of this finery is put to humorous use in the sequence in which the hapless troupers are forced to abandon their wardrobe trunks in the process of making their getaway from an Apache war party. The Indians are entranced by this mélange of colorful clothing which the actors left behind, and childishly don riotously mismatched combinations of costumes. The savage warriors of a moment before are thus transformed into a harmless group of kiddies displaying their Sunday best to each other.

In *Heller in Pink Tights*, as in all of Cukor's films about show people going all the way back to *The Royal Family of Broadway* (1930), his favorite theme of the conflict of reality and fantasy in people's lives is especially conspicuous, because, as stated before, entertainers must be aware of where the magic realm of illusion which they conjure up for others leaves off and the unglamorous world of everyday life begins, if they are themselves to remain in contact with reality.

For example, Tom Healy, Angelina's leading man (Anthony Quinn), does not like to admit that he has long since passed his prime as a matinee idol, so that he can go on playing romantic leads with the company. "In *La Belle Helénè*, I play Paris, the most handsome man in the world—with heavy makeup," he explains to a theater manager, reluctantly acknowledging that he and his fellow actors are getting older, though the parts they play are ageless. And Cukor underlines this point by contrasting how grotesque the garishly painted faces of Tom and some of the other older actors look up close while they are performing on stage, as opposed to how glowing and radiant they look from the audience's much more distant point of view.

In the movie's climax, reality and theatrical illusion equivalently overlap when Angelina allows Clint Mabry, a desperado, to escape from his enemies by substituting for her in the finale of a blood-and-thunder melodrama called *Mazeppa*. Wearing Angelina's costume and wig, and sitting astride a horse on the stage, the cowboy suddenly makes his steed jump across the footlights and gallop up the aisle and out of the theater—and out of the clutches of his real-life pursuers.

Mabry's escape from his foes while made up as the heroine of *Mazeppa* patently demonstrates a point often made in Cukor's films: that masquerade is not confined to the stage, since one way or another all of us can get caught up in role-playing in daily life. As the proprietress of a brothel says to Angelina when the latter introduces

Sophia Loren and Anthony Quinn sporting some of the outlandish costumes which Cukor's color consultant George Hoynigen-Heune turned up for Heller in Pink Tights, *which might be called Cukor's only "Western."*

herself as an actress, "We're all actresses, aren't we?" Similarly, the villain of the film, Mr. De Leon (played by silent film star Ramon Navarro), likes to make believe that he is a conventional businessman rather than a swindler, and dresses accordingly, complete with pince-nez and three-piece suit. Hence *Heller in Pink Tights*, along with *A Double Life* (1947), represents one of the most telling explorations in the whole Cukor canon of how fact and fantasy can become confused in life.

Heller is also among Cukor's most lighthearted entertainments; and, in keeping with the farcical tone of the proceedings, he stages the schmaltzy scenes from *Mazeppa* and *La Belle Helénè* seen in rehearsal or in performance during the movie with appropriate flamboyance and gusto. "I got Fritzi Massary, a great musical comedy genius, to coach Sophia as Helen of Troy in the scenes from the Offenbach operetta *La Belle Helénè*," says Cukor, just as many years before he had Fanny Brice help Claudette Colbert with the musical numbers in *Zaza* (1939). Sophia Loren is delightful in these scenes from *Mazeppa* and *Helénè*, and is really charming and quite funny all the way through the film, giving what is one of the most relaxed and ingratiating performances of any American film that she made.

Given the care that Cukor lavished on every aspect of the production, he was keenly hurt when he found out that Paramount had done some reediting of *Heller in Pink Tights* without his knowledge or consent. After he had spent five weeks personally supervising the editing of the film, the studio proceeded to cut the film in ways which only succeeded in making the development of the story line somewhat less clearly defined than it was in the final cut which Cukor had delivered to the front office.

In recalling the revisions made in *A Life of Her Own*, *Bhowani Junction*, as well as in *Heller* and other films that he has made, Cukor comments that when a director completes a movie in Hollywood "everyone in the studio thinks they have a right to take a shot at 'improving' it, right down to the doorman." Nevertheless, the harm done by the eleventh-hour alterations in *Heller in Pink Tights* is not substantial. The picture remains a disarmingly frivolous farce, and an unabashedly affectionate toast to the intrepid pioneers of American show business.

Although this chapter has focused on films which exemplify the splendid performances that Cukor has evoked from some of the great actresses of the screen, it is worth repeating that Cukor's charisma as an exceptionally skilled director of actors extends to performers of both sexes, as witnessed by the performances of actors like Robert Taylor, Jack Lemmon, and Aldo Ray, in the films discussed in this chapter. As Richard Roud wrote in the program notes for the Lincoln Center tribute to Cukor in 1978, Cukor knows how to direct actors and actresses "so as to achieve both good individual performances and tight ensemble playing."[13] Few directors, says Roud, have insisted as much as Cukor has upon the primordial importance of the screen actor as the basic raw material from which the movie maker must fashion his film. Joseph McBride would add that, because of Cukor's intense concentration on performance, perhaps no other director "can bring out so many nuances in an actor and capture an emotional state with such precision."[14]

Concerning Cukor's masterful handling of his stars, Norma Shearer's son, Irving Thalberg, Jr., has written to me, "I recall my mother's admiration for Cukor, and her feeling that he got top performances from her and many other actors and actresses."[15] Clearly Cukor's preoccupation with obtaining the best performances possible from his performers, as exemplified throughout this chapter, has paid off handsomely. Katharine Hepburn said it all when she remarked, "All the people in his pictures are as good as they can possibly be."[16]

5

From Page to Screen: Fiction on Film

BESIDES DIRECTING THE FILM VERSIONS of several stage plays, Cukor has also filmed a number of novels, some of which, like his film of Louisa May Alcott's *Little Women*, have been dealt with in earlier chapters. The present chapter will examine some of Cukor's screen versions of fictional works in order to contrast his method of filming fiction with his approach to filming a play, which was treated in Chapter 2.

To begin with, one might assume that drama is closer to film than fiction is, since a play, like a movie, is acted out; but there, essentially, the similarity ends. For both a novel and a film depend more on description and narration than on dialogue, while in a play the emphasis is reversed. Nevertheless, fiction and film still remain two very diverse mediums of artistic expression: inevitable differences arise between the manner in which a story can be told in a novel and on the screen. Thus compression becomes an important factor in making a movie from a novel, since the novelist can take as many pages as he pleases to develop his plot and characters, whereas the screen writer has only a couple of hours of screen time at his disposal to elaborate the same material.

Regardless of the superficial changes which a work of fiction must undergo in being transferred to the screen, however, the spirit, thematic intent, and overall thrust of the original story must be preserved in a film adaptation of a fictional work, if the film is to be reckoned a faithful adaptation of its literary source. This is not to say that the personal style of the director is not important, since he remains ultimately responsible for the overall quality and artistic unity of the motion-picture version of the novel he is filming. But a faithful rendition of a novel on film does require that he adapt his directorial style to the exigencies of the story which he is narrating on

W. C. Fields in one of his most beloved roles, Micawber in Dickens' David Copperfield (1935), with Freddie Bartholomeow as the young David.

film. As one movie director has remarked, a filmmaker has nothing to
direct until he has a story to tell. Let us see, then, with what success
Cukor has shaped some works of fiction into cinematic art.

David Copperfield (1935)

Cukor's screen version of Charles Dickens's *David Copperfield*
(1935) followed on his triumphant film adaptation of *Little Women*
(1933), which MGM loaned him to RKO to make with Katharine
Hepburn in the lead. *Copperfield* was produced at MGM by David
O. Selznick, for whom Cukor had already directed *Dinner At Eight*
(1933). Selznick encountered as much opposition at MGM when he
began planning the film version of *Copperfield* as he had experienced
at RKO when he set up the production of *Little Women* just prior to
moving to Metro. In spite of the critical and popular success of films
like *Little Women*, costume pictures based on literary classics were
still looked upon as risky ventures by studio executives because they
were so expensive to make. Eventually the front office at MGM
reluctantly gave Selznick the go-ahead on *Copperfield*, but he later
recalled that the opposition continued all the way through the production period, "and the entire studio thought I was going on my
nose."[1]

It is not surprising, then, that Cukor and Selznick failed to convince the front office to let them shoot the entire movie in Britain,
since the studio had not been enthusiastic about the project in the
first place. Hence the producer and director, along with screenwriter
Howard Estabrook, traveled to England before shooting began to
visit several sites associated with Dickens's life and with his
semiautobiographical novel. They returned to Hollywood with location footage that would furnish background shots which would establish the authentic English milieu of the story, as well as hundreds of
still photographs to guide the art department in designing the sets for
the film.

During their stay in England, Cukor and his companions engaged
the distinguished British novelist Hugh Walpole to contribute
dialogue to the screenplay, since Walpole possessed the knack of
devising dialogue passages that had a genuine Dickensian ring to
them. (He also played a cameo role in the movie as a vicar.)

Estabrook was responsible for the overall layout of the screenplay,
which retains the episodic structure of Dickens's rambling tale. The
second half of the novel is not as exciting as the first, and the same can

be said of the film. The problem is that David is a much more appealing character as a youngster than he is after he grows up to be a typical Victorian prig. Asked about this point, Cukor responds with another question: "If a writer like Dickens couldn't straighten out that difficulty satisfactorily, how could we have been expected to do it for him?" Cukor is a firm believer in the notion that capturing the essence of a classic novel on film involves accepting the book's flaws as well as its virtues, and then trusting in the original author's genius to carry the story along. The somewhat crude, melodramatic plot contrivances and the craggy, awkward structure of this vast, rather unwieldy novel give the book what Cukor calls "a kind of strength that one should not tamper with."[2]

Cukor's "warts-and-all" approach to filming *David Copperfield* issued in a faithful rendition of Dickens's work which *New York Times* critic Andre Sennwald termed "the most profoundly satisfying screen manipulation of a great novel that the camera has ever given us." It is astonishing, Sennwald continued, how many of the myriad incidents of David's life found their way into the film. Some of the episodes have admittedly been telescoped for the sake of brevity; but the movie nevertheless "encompasses the rich and kindly humanity of the original so brilliantly that it becomes a screen masterpiece in its own right."[3]

The *Times* critic also thought that the characters in the picture seemed to have stepped right out of Phiz's celebrated illustrations for the novel. The movie is especially deserving of this compliment, because Cukor and Selznick cast the picture with great care. Metro tried to foist a popular American child star of the day named Jackie Cooper on them to play David as a boy; but the pair insisted that the part should go to an English lad, Freddie Bartholomew.

Although W. C. Fields seems perfectly suited to the role of the eccentric Mr. Micawber, he was actually not the first choice for the part. "David Selznick wanted Charles Laughton for Micawber," says Cukor. "Laughton looked just great when he was made up for the role, but he didn't project Micawber's geniality or humanity; and he knew it. When Laughton finally withdrew after a few days of shooting, we asked Bill Fields to take over; but he was diffident at first about playing a straight character part because he was essentially a comedian." Cukor convinced him that he was born to play Micawber, however, since Fields's screen image as a bumbling, impecunious, erratic type was totally in keeping with Micawber's character.

"In his films Fields was forever being frustrated by inanimate objects," Cukor explains; "so I let him integrate a bit of this kind of comedy into his portrayal of Micawber. In the scene in which Micawber gets flustered while working at his tall bookkeeper's desk, Fields dipped his pen into a cup of tea instead of into the inkwell and stepped into the wastebasket as he walked away from the desk."

Fields's superb interpretation of Micawber, one of his best-loved roles, is but one of the finely wrought characterizations contributed to the film by the outstanding group of character actors assembled for the movie, including Basil Rathbone, Lionel Barrymore, and Roland Young, all of whom added immeasurably to the overall artistic excellence of the film. The movie opened to rave reviews and gratifying box-office receipts. Hence, when it came time for Selznick to bring Margaret Mitchell's monumental novel *Gone With the Wind* to the screen, Cukor was the logical choice to direct the picture, since by then he had proved his capability to mount handsome costume pictures like *Little Women* (1933) and *David Copperfield*.

Gone With the Wind (1939)

In the fall of 1936 Selznick announced that Cukor would direct *Gone With the Wind* (1939). As soon as Cukor finished *Camille* (1937), he began long-term preproduction work on the four-hour Civil War epic; and he continued his involvement in these preparations for more than two years, although he took time off along the way to direct *Holiday* (1938) and *Zaza* (1939). In his effort to recreate faithfully the novel's atmosphere of the Old South, an era gone with the winds of war, Cukor did background research and scouted locations in the South. He also conferred with Sydney Howard on the scenario, with William Cameron Menzies on the production design, and with Walter Plunkett on the costumes. In addition, he directed the screen tests and worked with Selznick on casting the picture.

Before principal photography began on January 26, 1939, Selznick hazarded that perhaps he should give a party before shooting started "to celebrate the last time when we're all talking to each other."[4] His facetious remark proved to be a sad prediction of crises to come. Before the film was finished, several major contributors to the movie had left the production, including cinematographer Lee Garmes and Cukor himself.

After three weeks' shooting on the film, Cukor was dismissed by Selznick on February 13, 1939. He was replaced the following day by

Victor Fleming, who was completing *The Wizard of Oz*, a picture that Cukor had passed up the chance to direct because he thought it a minor book freighted with third-rate imagery and because, ironically enough, he wanted to get on with the preparations for *Gone With the Wind*.

Lee Garmes has said that one of the major reasons why shooting was not progressing as well as it might have been during those first three weeks when Cukor was directing was most certainly Selznick's fault and not Cukor's. Prior to the start of filming, Garmes remembers that Selznick had virtually scrapped Howard's adaptation of the novel and written a new version of the script, in tandem with another screen writer, which was far less effective than Howard's original treatment of the material. "Cukor was too much of a gentleman," says Garmes, to tell Selznick that the revised script was "no fucking good."[5] When Fleming took over the direction of *Gone With the Wind*, however, he insisted that Selznick return to Howard's discarded scenario as the guiding principle for the final overhauling of the screenplay which was to be done with the assistance of Ben Hecht before shooting resumed on March 1, 1939. Selznick wisely complied with Fleming's demand.

If Selznick and not Cukor was to blame for the problems with which the production was plagued during the period that Cukor was directing the movie, what, then, was the reason for Cukor's dismissal by Selznick? Cutting through the gossip and speculation that has surrounded Cukor's removal from the film, Cukor himself says in retrospect that the principal reason why Victor Fleming replaced him was most likely that "Clark Gable took too seriously my reputation for being a good director of actresses."

Although Gable was a great screen personality, he lacked confidence in his acting abilities, Cukor continues; and the actor was therefore concerned that the director was favoring Vivien Leigh and Olivia de Havilland over him in the scenes that they played together, and that ultimately their performances would eclipse his own. Gable preferred Victor Fleming as Cukor's replacement, moreover, because Fleming had previously directed the actor opposite Jean Harlow in *Red Dust* (1932), one of Gable's best pictures up to that date. Cukor feels that it was utter nonsense for Gable to assume that he was giving too much attention to the movie's female stars, since it is always the text that dictates which characters should be highlighted in any one scene, not the whim of the director.

As for Selznick's willingness to substitute Fleming as director of the film at Gable's behest, Cukor comments that *Gone With the Wind* was the most ambitious picture Selznick had ever produced; he was consequently very nervous about it and also replaced other key people like Lee Garmes, whom Cukor regards as "one of the best cinematographers in the business."

Selznick's compulsive anxieties about the production were also evidenced in his wanting to attend the rehearsals of each scene, something which he had never wished to do before when working with Cukor. "Arthur Hornblow attempted to do the same thing when I was making *Gaslight* [1944]," Cukor recalls. "I refused in both cases, telling both men that they would have a chance to see each scene when they looked at the daily rushes, since that is the point at which the producer's criticism can be most valuable. After all, if Arthur or David knew all about directing a picture, why in the hell did they hire someone else to do it for them?"

In Selznick's case, the producer continued to offer elaborate, largely unhelpful suggestions about how a scene should be played. "I don't think that David ever gave up the idea that he could direct," says Cukor laconically; "but he couldn't."

In order to leave his stamp on the direction of the picture, however, Selznick continued to churn out longer and longer memos for Cukor on every conceivable subject, an obsessive and unsatisfactory method of dealing with directors which would get worse as the years went on, and eventually earned the producer the reputation in the industry of being "the great dictator." "I was irritated by all of those endless memos," says Cukor. "I asked David to call me on the telephone instead, but the memos kept coming anyhow. Alfred Hitchcock, who also directed some pictures for David, was furious when David's memos were published in book form. Hitch said that they should have published our answers as well!" As a matter of fact, Victor Fleming became so angry with Selznick's meddling in the direction of *Gone With the Wind* that he feigned sickness at one point, just to get some relief from Selznick's maddening interference in the direction of the film; and Sam Wood had to pinch-hit for Fleming for a brief period.

Gentleman that he is, Cukor for many years courteously denied reports that he secretly coached Vivien Leigh and Olivia de Havilland in their roles in *Gone With the Wind* after he left the picture, since he did not want to take any credit away from Victor Fleming. But the two actresses eventually spread the word. "When George Cukor was replaced," Olivia de Havilland has told me, "Vivien and I were beside ourselves because he had helped us establish the characters that we were playing."

Cukor directing Vivien Leigh and Clark Gable in the charity bazaar scene in Gone
with the Wind, *the scene he was directing when he was fired.*

At the first word of Cukor's dismissal, both actresses immediately
went to Selznick looking like widows in mourning, dressed as they
were in the black gowns they had been wearing in the war charity
bazaar scene, and futilely begged Selznick to reinstate Cukor. "During the subsequent months of shooting," Ms. de Havilland continues,
"whenever I would get nervous about how to play a scene that was
coming up the following week, I would call George and ask him if I
could go and see him over the weekend when we weren't shooting. I
felt so treacherous about Vivien not receiving the same help that I was
getting; but afterwards she told me that she had done the same
thing!"

Besides privately coaching Ms. Leigh and Ms. de Havilland in
their parts, Cukor has also left his mark on the movie by the very fact
that nearly everything that he shot was used in the final cut of the
film. The opening scene on the porch between Scarlett O'Hara
(Vivien Leigh) and the Tarleton twins, as finally edited, is probably a
combination of Cukor's version and Fleming's retake, but the other
material that Cukor filmed is all intact. This includes Mammy (Hattie
McDaniel) lacing up Scarlett's corset before the barbeque; Rhett

(Clark Gable) making Scarlett a present of a new hat from Paris; and Scarlett shooting the Union deserter who breaks into the house.[6] "I also shot the birthing of the baby that Melanie –Olivia de Havilland– brings forth with Scarlett's assistance," Cukor adds; "and the part of the charity bazaar sequence which I was filming when I was notified that I had been fired."

The night before he shot the childbirth sequence, Cukor sent Olivia de Havilland to a maternity ward to watch the delivery of a baby. "The next day, when we filmed the scene, I sat at the foot of the bed, just out of camera range, and twisted Olivia's ankle to make her wince every time she was supposed to have a labor pain." Recalling Cukor's efforts to make this and other scenes in the movie come to life, Ms. de Havilland says, "No other scenes in the film have the richness of detail that one finds in those which George Cukor directed."

In the last analysis, Cukor's creative influence permeates the film as a whole in that the extensive preproduction work he did on the film is reflected in every aspect of the mammoth production, right down to the tasteful set decorations. Musing about the enormous amount of time and energy he invested in *Gone With the Wind,* for which he received no screen credit whatever, Cukor says philosophically, "You know, I have never wasted time regretting setbacks of this kind. I am too much of a fatalist, or perhaps just too conceited for that. I have always felt that if I couldn't make one picture I would just make another. I have had too many disappointments in my time to bother holding grudges about any one of them. David and I parted painfully over *Gone With the Wind,* but it didn't hurt our friendship. Victor Fleming, on the other hand, was so bitter about his relationship with David on the film that he didn't even go to the premiere in Atlanta. But David and I remained friends."

For his part, Selznick remarked that Cukor's professional behavior throughout his association with the production, and even after he was replaced, was exemplary. "One of my most cherished mementoes of *Gone With the Wind* is an affectionate wire from George to me at the Atlanta opening, expressing his most fervent hopes for the picture's success," the producer has said. "I could wish that all people in the business behaved as well."[7]

When Garson Kanin's novel *Moviola* was turned into a three-part mini-series telecast in the spring of 1980, Cukor was portrayed by actor George Furth in the two-hour segment entitled *The Scarlett O'Hara Wars,* which treated the search for the leading actress for

Gone With the Wind. Cukor was amused that Furth received good notices for his depiction of one George Cukor as an energetic, resourceful, and reliable filmmaker. Cukor found the teleplay riddled with factual errors, however, but refused to make any official complaints to the network about the production on that score, although the late Mr. Selznick's family urged him to do so. "When you reach a certain age, you become more tolerant," he shrugs when discussing the matter. "One is therefore less willing to make a fuss about things that in the long run don't seem to matter much at this point." After all, *Gone With the Wind* will be remembered long after *Moviola* has been forgotten. So, for that matter, will George Cukor.

The Chapman Report (1962)

It was evident that MGM had not lost confidence in Cukor's directorial talents as a result of his being relieved of the director's post on *Gone With the Wind*, for he was immediately assigned to *The Women* (1939), a major movie with a spectacular cast of female stars. Some twenty years later Cukor made a film entitled *The Chapman Report* (1962), which has sometimes been called *The Women–II*, since it also boasts a host of top actresses, and like the earlier film is about the personal problems of a select group of ladies.

The Chapman Report examines in parallel fashion the private lives of a cross-section of suburban women who agree to participate in a sex survey in order to provide data for a latter-day Kinsey Report about the sexual mores of the American female. The film is based on a novel by Irving Wallace, whose lurid fiction a reviewer once dismissed as below the belt and beneath discussion; and as a book *The Chapman Report* is no exception in this regard. Nonetheless, after reading the novel, Cukor still thought it could be adapted to the screen with taste and discretion.

The first version of the screenplay, by Ron Alexander, was, if anything, even raunchier than the novel from which it was derived; and Cukor summarily rejected it as unscreenworthy. As it happened, Gene Allen, a first-class art director who worked on all of Cukor's color films from *A Star Is Born* (1954) through *My Fair Lady* (1964), was also something of a writer. He developed a workable scenario which possessed the taste and tact Alexander's script had lacked.

Cukor was making the film for Darryl Zanuck's independent production unit at Fox for distribution through Warner Brothers. Despite the fact that Darryl Zanuck had named his son Richard as official producer of the movie, the older Zanuck retained final say over the editing of the finished film, a situation I will return to later.

During preproduction planning, costume designer Orry-Kelly worked out in concert with Cukor a visual pattern for the costumes of the principal characters, according to which each woman's wardrobe would be dominated by one color that subtly characterized her personality and behavior. The frumpy Sarah Garnell (Shelley Winters), who is conducting an affair with a young lothario, usually wears black, as if subconsciously feigning a fictitious widowhood that would disassociate her from her marital ties; the fastidious Kathleen Barclay (Jane Fonda) is normally clothed in frosty white, which betokens her frigidity; the scatterbrained Teresa Harnish (Glynis Johns) is frequently dressed in tan, symbolizing that she gets no more than a little tarnished by her silly dalliances with men; and Naomi Shields (Claire Bloom) is most often clad in a much deeper brown, indicating that she is indelibly stained by her degrading nymphomania—in contrast to Teresa, whose frivolous behavior is but a pale reflection of Naomi's compulsive sexual promiscuity.

Cukor frequently photographs Naomi immersed in shadows, as a metaphor for the dark, furtive existence to which her grim obsession has condemned her. When a delivery boy (Chad Evertett) enters her home, Naomi provocatively entices the lad out of her brightly lit kitchen and into her bedroom, still darkened by drawn shades even in mid-morning, where she intends to seduce him. She ultimately cannot bring herself to corrupt this wholesome youth, however; instead she dispatches him from her murky lair and sends him out into the bright sunshine where he belongs. Later, when she finally reaches the depths of inner despair, Naomi withdraws for the last time into her shaded bedroom, where she washes down a bottle of pills with a swig of gin and plunges into the black abyss of death.

Cukor cast Claire Bloom against type as Naomi because he wanted to inject some pathos into the character by having the role played by an actress who radiated a classy, ladylike quality that would suggest that Naomi was once a woman of some respectability who had been reduced to her present wretched state by giving in to her ignoble drives, rather than a woman of easy virtue who had never been much more than a common harlot from the start. Ms. Bloom gives just the kind of performance that Cukor envisioned, with the result that Naomi comes across as the most complex character in the entire film. More than any other character in the movie the neurotic Naomi bears out the statement of one of Dr. Chapman's researchers that anyone can lose his way in the twisted corridors of his own mind; and, consequently, "in the last analysis everyone is sad."

After a successful preview in San Francisco, Cukor's final cut of the film was shipped to Darryl Zanuck, who was overseeing the shooting of *The Longest Day* (1962) in Europe; and Zanuck recut the film in his spare time to suit his own preferences. Needless to say, Zanuck's haphazard revisions in the film did more harm than good. "The original version was well-balanced," says Cukor; it was designed very deliberately to alternate "the most scabrous portions of the story with very delicate scenes."[8] By excising some of the more subdued passages of the film, Zanuck had unwittingly destroyed this delicate balance, so that the scenes depicting aberrant behavior were no longer as smoothly integrated into the fabric of the film as a whole, as they had been in the cut of the movie which Cukor had supervised.

Cukor accordingly warned Zanuck and his minions that once some of the particularly sensitive scenes that had added substance and seriousness to the film had been snipped out, the censors were going to assume that the movie was just as sensational as the book on which it was based, and call for cuts of their own in the scenes portraying sexual encounters, on the principle that these sequences were not adequately justified by a sufficiently meaningful context. And this is precisely what happened.

The sequence in which Naomi subconsciously entices a group of drunken musicians into raping her had been adroitly shot and judiciously edited. Yet the censors lopped off all but the beginning of the gang-rape footage, thereby severely diminishing the psychological significance of the scene, which is so important in establishing the self-hatred that motivates such masochistic behavior on Naomi's part, and which will finally lead to her suicide.

Teresa Harnish's abortive affair with a musclebound beach boy is the least important subplot in the film, since it basically serves as comic relief from the movie's more tragic episodes. Although the censors removed notable amounts of footage from other sections of the film, they left Teresa's story virtually untouched. Hence the portions of the movie devoted to Teresa take up a relatively larger percentage of screen time in the movie as a whole than Cukor had planned, with the result that Teresa appears to be a more important character in the overall scheme of the film than she actually is. Consequently, the censor board managed to throw the film further out of balance than even Zanuck had done. Even in its final truncated form, however, *The Chapman Report* proves Cukor to be a thoroughgoing alchemist, since the movie emerges as unquestionably more thought-provoking and sophisticated that the salacious novel on which it was based, as is evident just from his touching handling of the Naomi character alone.

Justine (1969)

In contrast to *The Chapman Report, Justine* was based on a respected modern classic, *The Alexandria Quartet,* a four-volume work of fiction by Lawrence Durrell that presents a rich tapestry of life in Alexandria in the 1930s. After Fox had purchased the screen rights to this *magnum opus,* the project was at first entrusted to writer-director Joseph Mankiewicz and producer Walter Wanger; but following the troubles Fox had with both of them over *Cleopatra* (1963), the studio repossessed the property and eventually turned it over to writer Lawrence Marcus, producer Pandro Berman, and director Joseph Strick, noted for his film of Joyce's *Ulysses* (1967). After several weeks of unsatisfactory location work in Tunisia with relatively little usable footage to show for it, Strick, too, was fired. Producer Berman, who had already made *Sylvia Scarlett* (1936) and *Bhowani Junction* (1956) with Cukor, asked Cukor to take over the direction of the picture, which was to be finished on the Fox lot back in Hollywood.

Justine is, among other things, a bizarre tale of sexual ambiguity. During the credits of *Justine,* Melissa, a belly dancer (Anna Karina), is seen dancing in a smoky dive backed up by three chorines who are unveiled at the conclusion of their number as transvestite homosexuals. Right from the start we infer that things and people are not always what they seem in the exotic, corrupt city of Alexandria, teeming as it is with romantic and political intrigue.

The film continues to develop this Cukorian theme of illusion versus reality, as we realize how many of the characters are pretending to be what they are not. Pursewarden, the distinguished first secretary of the British embassy in Alexandria (Dirk Bogarde), masquerades as a lady's man, but is really a wretched homosexual who can only make heterosexual love to his own blind sister Liza.

The bewitching temptress Justine (Anouk Aimée) surrounds herself with a spurious air of tragedy by periodically searching the child brothels of the city for a kidnapped daughter who Pursewarden shrewdly suspects never existed. The carefully nurtured fable of her long-lost little girl enables the promiscuous Justine to insinuate herself into the sympathies and affections of several unsuspecting males

Michael York as Darley makes love to Anouk Aimée in the title role of Justine *(1969).*

whom she wishes to seduce, including the naive British school-teacher Darley (Michael York). On a deeper level, the phantom child whom Justine fruitlessly seeks in the child brothels more than likely represents her own vanished youthful innocence, which she lost under similar circumstances, and which, of course, she can never reclaim.

At one point Pursewarden scoffs at her pretensions of being a self-styled tragic goddess of love by assuring her that even if he were not homosexual he would in any event never have elected to pass through her sexual turnstile. "When are you going to cease being a sin cushion, into which we must all thrust our rusty pins?" he asks her pointedly.

But Justine, like so many other characters in the film, continues to take refuge in various kinds of pretense whenever it suits her purposes. In order to suggest visually how she systematically cultivates a false facade, Justine is shown striking poses before a four-sided mirror, and later exchanging masks with a male homosexual at a costume ball. Conversely, Pursewarden becomes completely fed up with the vile world of deception of which he is a part, and swallows poison in a final, desperate fit of depression. In this suicide scene Dirk Bogarde puts the finishing touches on a brilliant performance that overshadows all the others in the film.

Although Cukor shies away from taking over the direction of a film which he did not prepare for production, one of the reasons that he accepted this belated assignment was the opportunity it gave him to work with an actor of Bogarde's artistry. Still Cukor would have preferred to have had something to say about casting some of the other parts in the picture, such as the role of Justine. He found Anouk Aimée too cold and remote to suggest the seductive power which Justine possessed to ignite men's desires, and he never succeeded to his satisfaction in making the inscrutable actress warm up to her role.

Cukor would also have liked to have shot the location scenes himself, since at times it was difficult to match the footage which Strick had filmed in Tunisia with additional material for the same scene which Cukor later photographed in the studio back in Hollywood. "It is frightfully difficult to work in this piecemeal fashion," Cukor comments. "You just have to pull things together as best you can."

Cukor's arduous efforts to create a coherent movie out of a complex script based on a four-volume novel was not helped by the final editing of the picture. At the time he took over the picture, *Justine* was planned as a major production which would run close to three hours when it was finished; and a first assemblage of the footage yielded a film of approximately that length. The front office decided to shorten the film to a more conventional running time of just under two hours, however; and consequently the movie was drastically condensed, to the point where the continuity of the plot is sometimes hard to follow. (Darley's voice-over narration, added to tie the story together, helps, but not enough.)

For example, a sequence was apparently hacked out of the film in which a letter from Pursewarden is read aloud to his blind sister Liza which confirms for the viewer the incestuous nature of their relationship. Because this scene is missing in the release prints of the picture, the filmgoer continues to be confused about this crucial point until it is at last clarified in another scene much later in the movie. Once more, as in the case of Cukor films like *The Chapman Report*, attempts by the front office to revise one of his pictures did not produce a better final cut than the one which Cukor had himself approved.

Justine also recalls *The Chapman Report* in that the present film is likewise noteworthy for the discretion with which Cukor depicts sordid situations. When confronted with the problem of shooting a scene in a child brothel, Cukor judged it improper to employ real children inside the brothel. Instead he established the perverse nature of the place by showing a group of real little girls gathered outside the entrance, implying that they were on the inside, too. For the interior scenes, however, he substituted female midgets wearing veils for the actual children seen in the exterior shots, and placed dolls and other trinkets around the interior set to imply not only the tender age of these pathetic prostitutes, but also to suggest how these wretched children were being robbed of their youth and innocence by the heartless adults who exploited them. With his customary utilization of artistic indirection, Cukor was able to wring pathos from a scene that could in other, less sensitive hands have been merely revolting.

Travels with My Aunt (1972)

Cukor's next film was also an adaptation of a work by a major twentieth-century British novelist: *Travels with My Aunt* (1972), based on the novel by Graham Greene. When Cukor had just embarked on preliminary preparations for filming, he wrote that "we're sparing no effort to do right by Greene's most amusing book."[9]

Greene's comic heroine Aunt Augusta is a shameless old lady with a deliciously wicked past who takes it upon herself to initiate her inhibited middle-aged nephew Henry Pulling into the more exciting side of life by shepherding him around the world on a tour which includes some places not listed in the guidebooks.

In the course of their journey they also meet up with some equally strange people, such as the nefarious Mr. Visconti, an old beau of Aunt Augusta's, for whom she still carries a torch, despite the fact that he has deserted her several times over the years.

"I think the book is a rare combination of robust adventure and really funny comedy," says Cukor in discussing *Travels with My Aunt*. "Greene created some very rich and marvelous characters in the story; the warmth and range of both the elderly aunt and her nephew are what primarily attracted me to the subject in the first place." He adds that even before Jay Presson Allen, the principal author of the screenplay, started to work on the script, he "went through the novel and cross-referenced all the episodes, so that every incident of importance in the story would turn up somewhere in the picture. But there just wasn't room for everything. The wonderful scene where Aunt Augusta's old lover Visconti masquerades as a priest to get out of a jam, for example, had to be left out."

During the script conferences, Cukor continues, "Jay Allen and I often compared a scene in the screenplay with the way Greene had written it in the book, and used as much of the dialogue from the novel as possible. We clung very much to the spirit of the novel, and made changes reluctantly and only in the interest of dramatizing the story more vividly."

One such alteration occurs at the finale, and for Greene this change contributed to what he terms the movie's "misinterpretation" of his original story. In correspondence Greene has said, "When I read the script that was smuggled to me from Spain" where Cukor's unit was doing location work, "I was horrified."[10]

"Greene's ending to the story is more hardbitten than the one in the film," Cukor concedes. "In the novel the aging Visconti is going to marry a twelve-year-old girl in South America and desert Aunt Augusta once more, even though she still loves him. In the movie, on the other hand, we show her at long last becoming disenchanted with Visconti, and thereby being released from the thrall of her lifelong infatuation with him—something which Greene, perhaps with greater truth and realism, does not allow to happen in the novel." In permitting Aunt Augusta's crude awakening to Visconti's duplicity in the film, it is clear that Cukor has altered Greene's original ending in a manner which in fact brings it implicitly more into line with his own personal vision about the necessity for reality to triumph over illusion in people's lives.

"Our ending is more lighthearted than Greene's," Cukor explains. "Henry flips a coin to decide whether or not he is going to continue living under Aunt Augusta's tutelage or go back to his bank job; and we end with the coin frozen in mid-air, tantalizing the audience to conjecture about whether or not he will continue on his spree with her. Chances are that he will," since he has already come this far with her. Indeed, by film's end, Henry seems to have become fairly used to Aunt Augusta's cavalier way of life, summed up so aptly in her remark that "some of us are able to get out of life what everyone else is willing to put into it."

In addition to having serious reservations about the film's denouement, Greene likewise was unhappy with the casting of Maggie Smith in the role of Aunt Augusta because in his view she was "much too young."[11] "There were two ways of approaching the role of Aunt Augusta," Cukor responds. "One was to get a woman closer to the age of this elderly lady and try to make her look younger in the flashbacks to Augusta's youth," when she first met and fell in love with Visconti. That was the route that Cukor would have gone had Katharine Hepburn played the role, as originally planned. But Ms. Hepburn left the picture before shooting started because of disagreements over various aspects of the production with studio officials who thought her too bossy. "The other way to cast the part," Cukor continues, "was to choose a younger actress with the flashbacks in mind, and then age her for the scenes in the present. In giving the part to Maggie Smith, of course, we opted for the latter way of handling the role. She was perfectly fine and got an Oscar nomination for her performance."

Another problem, Cukor notes, was how Augusta's shy nephew Henry should be played. "Alec McCowen was absolutely right in not playing Henry as a fuddy duddy, but in making him more sympathetic, so that the audience could identify with him more easily."

In reviewing the film for *Time*, Jay Cocks wrote, "*Travels* is in the easefully luxurious style of its director, whose sense of subdued but splendid theatricality is everywhere in evidence, from the meticulous *mise en scène* and the unobtrusive movement of the camera to the careful, practiced composition of every scene. (Cukor stashes a bouquet in the corner to balance the frame the way Aunt Augusta might bedeck her room with roses.)"[12]

"I wasn't aware of trying to fill the entire wide screen frame all of the time," Cukor comments. "This kind of thing can look very self-conscious and 'arranged' if it is overdone. I try to make the composition and the cutting as unostentatious as possible, since too much technical windowdressing can sometimes be a mere coverup for a lack of intensity in a film. With Greene's story and the cast we had, there was no need to worry about a lack of intensity."

Novelists like Graham Greene may on occasion register complaints about Cukor's screen versions of their fiction, but by and large Cukor's movies of the novels examined in this chapter and elsewhere in this book demonstrate his efforts to make faithful screen adaptations of fictional works. In some cases, like *The Chapman Report*, Cukor's movie is better than the book from which it was derived.

"I've always tried to do the best I could," he says, "to preserve the essence and spirit of a novel on film, though I may not always have succeeded in doing so." In the case of films like *David Copperfield* and the Hepburn *Little Women*, he succeeded supremely well.

6

Make Mine Music:
The Musical Films

FOR A MAN WHO CLAIMS THAT HE CANNOT carry a tune and has never truly felt at home making musicals, Cukor has directed a couple of the best musical motion pictures ever made including *A Star Is Born* (1954) and *My Fair Lady* (1964). Though his other musicals do not belong in this exalted company, all of them are diverting, eye-filling, entertaining movies.

What Price Hollywood? (1932)

Zaza (1939) and *Heller in Pink Tights* (1960) are not usually numbered among his musicals because, although each contains a couple of musical numbers, they do not qualify as full-blown musical films. They are dealt with in other chapters of this book. *What Price Hollywood?*, on the other hand, is not a musical at all; yet it is treated in this chapter because it was the ultimate source of Cukor's musical film *A Star Is Born* (1954). *What Price Hollywood?* first served as the basis of the 1937 *A Star Is Born* directed by William Wellman, which Cukor in turn remade as a musical. There are some differences between *What Price Hollywood?* and its two later incarnations as *A Star Is Born* in 1937 and 1954; but the story line is fundamentally the same in all three versions.

In *What Price Hollywood?* Constance Bennett plays Mary Evans, a young hopeful who achieves stardom with the help of Maximillian Carey (Lowell Sherman), an alcoholic director whose career is taking a nosedive at the same rapid pace that Mary's is taking off. Constance Bennett is fine as Mary, and Cukor cast her in three more films in the following decade; but the picture really belongs to Lowell Sherman, who makes Max Carey a likable as well as a tragic figure. After establishing himself as an actor in silent movies like D. W. Griffith's

Audrey Hepburn and Rex Harrison in My Fair Lady *(1964), for which both Harrison and George Cukor won Oscars.*

Way Down East (1920), Sherman had gone on to become a director of some note, and in fact would direct Katharine Hepburn in her Oscar-winning performance in *Morning Glory* (1933) soon after he finished his acting assignment in *What Price Hollywood?* (Gregory Ratoff, who plays a studio boss in the present film, also became a director as well as an actor later on.)

It was a stroke of genius to have Carey played by an actor who was himself also a director in his own right, for Sherman's personal experience as a director enables him to handle the scenes in which Carey directs Mary Evans with an authority and a professional polish that makes the viewer readily believe that Carey is quite capable of transforming Mary into the movie star she shortly becomes under his mentorship. To the scenes which chart Carey's quick decline into alcoholism, moreover, Sherman brings a touch of the self-mockery which characterized his brother-in-law John Barrymore's playing of similar drunk scenes, most notably in Cukor's *Dinner at Eight* (1933).

Sherman sometimes appeared in the films which he also directed, such as *High Stakes* (1931); but he never gave a better performance than under the guidance of fellow director George Cukor in *What Price Hollywood?* His suicide scene alone is enough to confirm this statement. After bailing Carey out of the drunk tank, Mary puts him to bed for the night in her own home. As she leaves the bedroom, she snaps off the light, leaving him in darkness. Then Carey, as Joseph McBride describes the scene, "raises his hand and lets the sash of her dress trail through his fingers." For Carey, already considering suicide, this moment represents "the slipping away of everything he cares about."[1]

Contemplating the eclipse of his career plunges Carey into a deeper darkness than that of the room in which he lies. He leaves his bed and restlessly rummages around the room looking for liquor, until he happens upon a revolver in a bureau drawer. Now that the instrument of his self-destruction has conveniently fallen into his hands, he studies his haggard face in the mirror while he summons the courage to make use of the gun. Then he notices a picture of himself taken in better days: the contrast between the debonair face represented in the photograph and the ravaged visage framed in the mirror before him is too painful to behold, and clinches his resolve to do away with himself.

A succession of shots that recapitulate Carey's steady slide into degradation is superimposed on his anguished countenance, while the sound track emits a grating, pulsating sound that suggests the turmoil raging inside his skull at this fateful moment. Finally he pulls the trigger and, while being photographed in slow motion, falls forward and dies. McBride ends his lengthy analysis of this sequence by rightly calling it a masterpiece of both acting and direction that caps Sherman's fine performance in the film. It is all the more tragic that, after reaching the peak of his acting career in *What Price Hollywood?*, Lowell Sherman died prematurely a scant two years later while still in his late forties.

What Price Hollywood? was the first Cukor film which Selznick produced. It was made right after the director joined the producer at RKO. At one stage Selznick had thought of the project, initially titled *The Truth about Hollywood*, as a possible vehicle for Clara Bow's comeback; but the production instead evolved into the film that Cukor made. The movie was close to Selznick's heart, says Cukor, because he believed that it really gave a true picture of the film colony. In pairing the rise of Mary Evans with the fall of Max Carey, the film honestly tried to show both the pleasant and unpleasant sides of the movie capital. And since the film did fairly well critically and financially, Selznick decided to remake it less than five years later as *A Star is Born*, with William Wellman as director.

The story was extensively retooled for the new version, with the alcoholic director replaced by an alcoholic actor named Norman Maine (Fredric March), who marries the heroine, Vicki Lester (Janet Gaynor), after helping her to achieve stardom. It is interesting to note how incidents that are only referred to in *What Price Hollywood?* are developed in depth in *A Star Is Born*. For example, in *Hollywood* a newspaper headline announces that Mary Evans has won an Academy Award. In *Star Is Born* this item is expanded into a major sequence in which the event is spoiled by the appearance at the ceremonies of the heroine's drunken actor-husband, loudly proclaiming that he deserves an award for having made the worst picture of the year.

The artistic demise of Max Carey as a director in *What Price Hollywood?* had been suggested by the career of Marshall Neilan, who hit the skids in the sound era after directing some successful silent films starring Mary Pickford. By the same token, Norman Maine, the corresponding character in *A Star Is Born*, was inspired by movie actor John Bowers, the husband of actress Marguerite de la Motte, whose career foundered after talking pictures came in. Bowers drowned in the Pacific in 1936, an apparent suicide; but there is no doubt that Norman Maine's drowning in *A Star Is Born* is clearly intentional.

Norman Maine was also to some degree modeled on John Barrymore, and one incident in the film in particular was based on an encounter Cukor had had with the actor. "After Jack Barrymore did so well as Mercutio in *Romeo and Juliet* (1936), I wanted him to play the baron in *Camille* (1937), the part finally taken by Henry Daniell," Cukor remembers. "So I went to see him in the depressing rest home where he was drying out at the time. He was comic and sad at one and the same time while we talked in the dreary sitting room in the presence of his male nurse Kelly. He told me for instance that I need not fear that some lunatic was going to suddenly appear and announce that he was Napoleon right in the middle of our chat. When I came back from my visit with Jack, I stopped to see David Selznick and Bill Wellman, the director of *A Star Is Born*, and recounted this bittersweet tale to them. They wrote the incident right into their picture as a scene for Freddie March to play, and I used it in my version of *A Star Is Born* as well."

It is one of the ironies of film history, incidentally, that Fredric March, who had hilariously mimicked John Barrymore in Cukor's *The Royal Family of Broadway* (1931), would only a few years later play a role in the Selznick *Star Is Born* inspired to some extent by Barrymore's tragic descent into alcoholism.

A Star Is Born (1954)

As noted above, the screenplay of the 1937 *A Star Is Born*, which had been elaborated from the script of the 1932 Cukor film *What Price Hollywood?*, in turn became the basis of Cukor's own 1954 musical remake of the same story, marking the only time in Cukor's career that he filmed for a second time a story that he had done on the screen before. "I am a little wary of doing remakes," says Cukor, "because you have to fight the memory that moviegoers have of what was done before. There has to be some compelling reason for making a picture all over again, such as the addition of songs, as in the case of *A Star Is Born*. You must also be careful that the strengths of the material you are reworking do not get lost in the remake." One virtue of the earlier versions of *A Star Is Born* was the strong story line, and Moss Hart preserved the powerful dramatic values of the plot in his new screenplay.

The one time Cukor repeated himself: (top) Constance Bennett with Lowell Sherman in What Price Hollywood? *(1932); (bottom) Judy Garland solo in the last scene of* A Star Is Born *(1954), the second remake of the earlier film.*

Norman (James Mason) is not consciously jealous of the flourishing career of his wife, Vicki (Judy Garland), but her success in pictures does serve to underscore his own ignominious decline as a movie idol. He tries to sweeten this bitter reality by living most of the time in an alcoholic haze from which Vicki is finally powerless to rescue him. Nonetheless, she never ceases to love him.

After Norman's suicide she introduces herself proudly, with tears welling up in her eyes, to a packed auditorium that has come to hear Vicki Lester sing, as "Mrs. Norman Maine"—as if to emphasize that she has no intention of disassociating herself from Norman in death any more than she did in life. This is undoubtedly one of the most moving finales of any Cukor film, and puts the finishing touch to Judy Garland's superb portrayal of Vicki, a girl who keeps herself firmly rooted in reality while caught up in the fantasy world of motion picture making, but who was unable to help her husband to do the same.

A Star Is Born was Cukor's first film in color (aside from the scenes of *Gone With the Wind* [1939] he shot) and wide screen (aside from the opening sequence of *The Actress* [1953]).

In filming *A Star is Born* he proved himself to be one of the first film directors to use the wide screen intelligently, even though from the beginning he disliked its unfortunate mail-slot shape. "When the wide screen was introduced," Cukor recalls, "the situation was similar to that which occurred at the time that the talkies came in, many movie makers lost their heads and started throwing out the window everything they had learned in the silent days about moving pictures being a visual medium just because of the advent of sound. Similarly, the day I began shooting *A Star Is Born* at Warners, the technical people told me that I must forget everything I had known in the past about composing shots because of the new wide screen format. They said that the wide screen lens lacked the depth of focus of the ordinary camera lens I was familiar with, and that therefore I must line up the actors right in front of the camera at all times because anyone placed even a short distance away from the camera would automatically go out of focus.

"I shot the way the technicians wanted me to for exactly one day; and then I said, 'To hell with it! I can't abandon everything I have ever known about making movies just because of some damned new process.' After that I went ahead and composed each shot precisely the way I always have, and everything worked out all right."

Cukor made no attempt to keep the action centered symmetrically in mid-screen, as had often been customary in wide-screen films at that time. Rather he allowed the action to move from one side of the screen to the other, thus using to best advantage the increased space available in the new format. When Judy Garland sings the torchy "The Man Who Got Away" in a small nightclub after hours, Cukor has the camera follow her as she roams around, sometimes almost disappearing out of the frame. Ms. Garland is rarely in the center of the screen during the number, and this very lack of perfect pictorial composition makes the scene seem more dynamic and spontaneous, Cukor feels.

Moreover, Cukor created compositions for the wide screen that would not have been nearly so effective on a conventional movie screen. As one critic pointed out, Cukor at times positioned Norman and Vicki at opposite ends of the wide screen, with only empty space between them, in order to suggest visually their growing isolation from one another.

Cukor matched his innovative use of wide screen in *A Star Is Born* by likewise setting new standards for the employment of color in this, his first color feature. The latter accomplishment was achieved with the assistance of production designer Gene Allen and color consultant George Hoynigen-Huene, both of whom, as noted earlier, collaborated on several of Cukor's color films, beginning with *A Star Is Born* and continuing onward during the next decade. Working in tandem with these two invaluable associates, "Cukor eliminated the bright, garish reds, greens, and yellows which dominated most technicolor productions of the time," writes Allen Estrin, "and replaced them with softer hues like browns, light blues, and pinks to give the film a much more realistic, 'natural' look."[2]

The film might have been aptly entitled "A Star Is Reborn," in that it marked the auspicious return to the screen of Judy Garland, whose movie career had fared no better than Norman Maine's after she was replaced by Betty Hutton in *Annie Get Your Gun* (1950). Because *A Star Is Born* was Ms. Garland's crucial comeback film, Cukor often had to reassure his nervous star about the myriad anxieties which plagued her during shooting, not the least of which was her fluctuating weight. "She just seemed to swell up at times," Cukor remembers, probably because of neglecting her diet when she felt particularly under stress. "Since she did not want to work unless she looked her best, we would have to adjust her costumes so that the periodic

variations in her weight would not be too apparent on the screen."
Unexpected complications of this kind explain why it took Cukor
longer to make the movie than originally anticipated.

Her role in *Star Is Born* was especially important for Judy Garland's subsequent career in movies, Cukor points out, "because the
film was the beginning of Judy's career as a real actress. Since she'd
never done such a serious picture before, she had never even cried on
the screen until she made *Star Is Born*. But once we got going, she
found within herself the capacity to do dramatic scenes; and she
continued to take on serious roles from then on. "It was a terrible
thing that Judy Garland and James Mason did not get Oscars for their
work in the film," Cukor adds, "since both of them were nominated
and certainly deserved to win."

In sum, *A Star Is Born* is a splendid blend of song and story, with
the Harold Arlen–Ira Gershwin songs carefully integrated into the
plot in a way that keeps the film from becoming an episodic "backstage musical." After Norman's suicide, the viewer realizes in retrospect that Vicki's rendition of "The Man Who Got Away" earlier in the
picture was really a subtle foreshadowing of her inevitable loss of
Norman; in a similar manner the story adds an extra dimension to
some of the other numbers in the movie as well.

Because of this careful meshing of the plot and musical score in the
film, one would have thought the studio would have been satisfied
with the picture when Cukor finished it. Perhaps because the front
office thought the tone of the film too heavy for a musical, they
inserted a lengthy production number called "Born in a Trunk" into
the completed film without Cukor's knowledge, after he had departed for a European vacation. This elaborate musical interlude,
which was created by the movie's choreographer, Richard Barstow,
brought the total running time of the film to about three hours.

When Cukor later saw the expanded version of the film at a
preview, he felt that the movie was now too long, and asked that he
and script writer Moss Hart be allowed to trim away enough footage
to compensate for the interpolation of "Born in a Trunk" into the
movie. But Cukor's offer was courteously declined, on the grounds
that the film required no revisions whatever. After the movie had
opened and Cukor had gone to India to make *Bhowani Junction*
(1956), however, studio officials decided to carve twenty minutes or
so out of the movie in order to make possible an additional daily
showing of the picture at the theaters where it played, thereby
increasing the film's revenue.

Today Cukor is philosophical about this tampering with his film,
since *A Star Is Born* has a secure reputation as a classic musical. But

he still feels that he and Moss Hart would have done a smoother job of shortening the film. "Had we been allowed, Moss Hart and I could have shaved away twenty minutes from the film which would have been imperceptible to the audience," Cukor contends. Instead the studio chopped out whole scenes to bring the running time of the film down to a little more than two and a half hours. One scene in particular is a special loss. In it Norman proposes to Vicki in the recording studio where the dubbing of the songs for one of Vicki's films is in progress. When the recording of one of her numbers is played back, Norman's tender proposal to Vicki, made while the microphone was still on, comes booming over the loudspeaker to the delight and embarrassment of both of them.

Among the other casualties of the cutting that the front office ordered to make room for the *"Born in a Trunk"* number is, ironically enough, another song, the cheery "Lose That Long Face," which Vicki must sing with great gusto and gaiety in a scene in a musical film she is shooting, despite the fact that she is worried about losing Norman for good at the time. No wonder that Bosley Crowther wrote an angry piece in the *New York Times* entitled "A Star Is Shorn," expressing his dismay after the movie opened that Warners had cut the film. He would have been even more perturbed had he known that the portions of the film's original negative containing the deleted sections of the movie would eventually be melted down in order to extract the silver they contained, and that therefore these segments would be lost forever.

Nonetheless, *A Star Is Born* in its final form was not marred in any essential way by Warners' meddling with the movie; it was a good enough picture that no amount of studio interference could keep it from being the grand movie musical that it is. (*A Life of Her Own* [1950], *The Chapman Report* [1962], and *Justine* [1969] are the Cukor films most hurt by studio-imposed recutting.) One only has to consider the inferior 1976 remake of *A Star Is Born*, recast this time as a rock musical for Barbra Streisand, to appreciate anew the worth of Cukor's musical version of this oft-told tale, unquestionably the most enduring version of them all.

Les Girls (1957)

Cukor's second musical, *Les Girls*, is perhaps the most explicit of all his films in dealing with the conflict of fact and fantasy in people's lives. In *Les* (pronounced *Lay*) *Girls* the same events are shown in flashback from three different points of view. Each rendition of the facts, though differing markedly from the others, revolves around the common past shared by show girls Sybil Wren (Kay Kendall), Joy Henderson (Mitzi Gaynor), and Angele Ducros (Tania Elg), and their lead dancer Barry Nichols (Gene Kelly). When Sybil writes a book about their experiences together as troupers, Angele sues her for libel.

In giving their contrary testimonies, Sybil and Angele individually "remember" their mutual past in a way that projects a somewhat romanticized self-image of each of them. It remains for Barry to give a relatively unvarnished account of the various romantic entanglements which they had during the period in which they were all touring Europe together with their song and dance act which they called "Les Girls."

Because each of the witnesses is allowed "equal time" to express his or her own version of what happened, it would seem that Cukor is sympathetic to the way that each of them in varying degrees has subconsciously revised the common experience in a manner that enables each to cope more adequately with the past in the present. As Andrew Sarris puts it, Cukor does not imply that people are essentially liars; only that everyone tends to tell the truth in their own peculiar fashion. In fact, throughout the film an old man passes by the court house carrying a sign that asks, "What is truth?"

In the end Cukor leaves the verdict to the audience, since the judge (Henry Daniell) cannot himself decide in favor of either the defendant or the plaintiff. Consequently the movie winds up with Angele dropping her charges and Barry winning Joy, the least glamorous but most sensible girl of the group. In choosing Joy, Barry is opting for a down-to-earth individual who represents the superiority of reality over illusion, a telling decision that is very much in harmony with Cukor's treatment of this theme throughout the film.

Because big, expensive musicals were not attracting audiences in the late 1950s in the way that they did a little earlier, MGM did not use all of the songs which Cole Porter wrote for the film, so that greater attention could be given to the comic twists of the plot. (Kay Kendall's hilarious drunk scene, in which she sneaks drinks from bottles labeled cough medicine and perfume, is screen comedy at its best.) Although the great composer had passed his peak, those numbers that were mounted in the film, such as the delightfully wicked "Ladies in Waiting," are fine; and one therefore misses songs like "High Flying Wings on My Shoes," which surely could have provided Gene Kelly with a satisfying dance routine. Nevertheless *Les*

Girls, like *A Star Is Born,* merits a special place among musical films as an original musical created directly for the screen and not adapted from a Broadway show.

Let's Make Love (1960)

Let's Make Love is also an original movie musical, but it does not measure up to the standard Cukor had set for himself in his previous two musical films. The reason is that the slender story line is far too insubstantial to provide sufficient support even for a light musical comedy like this one.

The predictable plot is woven around the attempt of billionaire Jean-Marc Clement (Yves Montand) to pass himself off to Amanda Dell, an aspiring off-Broadway performer (Marilyn Monroe), as another struggling neophyte like herself. Because the movie was designed primarily as a vehicle for Ms. Monroe, Gregory Peck had turned down the role of Jean-Marc; and it was then offered to Montand, whose experience as a song-and-dance man made him a better choice for the part anyway. Montand is at his best in the scenes in which Jean-Marc takes lessons from Bing Crosby, Gene Kelly, and Milton Berle (all of whom appear as themselves in the movie) in singing, dancing, and telling jokes.

Ms. Monroe's best moment in the movie is her steamy rendering of the old Cole Porter standard "My Heart Belongs to Daddy," Amanda's big song in the show she is rehearsing. She performs it in the full glare of a bank of blazing spotlights which symbolizes how Amanda is bedazzling Jean-Marc as he watches from the sidelines. While seductively purring Porter's naughty lyrics, she glides around the stage among the male chorus like a predatory jungle cat on the prowl for a mate; yet the whole number comes off as more funny than racy. "Marilyn was a charming comedienne," says Cukor; and she shared with Jean Harlow the ability to deliver a *double-entendre* with a wide-eyed look of innocence that implied that she did not fully grasp its saucy implications. "And that," Cukor concludes, "made it all the funnier."

Never before had Ms. Monroe been as agreeable in working as she was with Cukor while shooting *Let's Make Love.* Asked how he managed to get on with her as well as he did, Cukor answers, "I didn't try to treat her like I was her sugar daddy or to win her with my baby-blue eyes. I just tried to create a climate in which she felt at ease

Glamour!: (top), Marilyn Monroe on the set of Let's Make Love *(1960), with Cukor, one of the few directors she was willing to work with; (bottom) Gene Kelly with his dancing troupe in* Les Girls *(1957), Tania Elg, Mitzi Gaynor and Kay Kendall.*

and found it possible to work. She knew that I could help her deliver the goods if she trusted me."

Nonetheless, Ms. Monroe could still make the going rough. Her growing psychic instability was manifested by the enormous amount of time it took to rehearse and shoot her key song in the film, "My Heart Belongs to Daddy." She associated the lyrics, it seems, with her first husband Jim Dougherty, whom she had called "daddy," and with her current husband, Arthur Miller, whom she often addressed as "papa." Because of the acutely private emotions the song evoked in her, and her corresponding unwillingness to work on it, the six-minute production number took eleven days to shoot.

In addition to Ms. Monroe's emotional problems, Cukor also had to cope with her chronic tardiness and her incapacity to master her lines. Because she could only remember one snippet of dialogue at a time, Cukor, who favors long takes, was reduced to filming her dialogue scenes in a succession of brief shots. Curiously enough, says Cukor, when all of these bits and pieces were strung together in the editing room, somehow a complete performance emerged.

Something's Got to Give (1962)

As a kind of epilogue to the Cukor-Monroe *Let's Make Love,* I should take up the only other film on which they collaborated, *Something's Got to Give,* a remake, with one or two songs added, of *My Favorite Wife* (1940). The original version, directed by Garson Kanin with Irene Dunne and Cary Grant in the leads, was a chic romp about a wife long thought dead who resurfaces after her hapless husband has married a second time. Cukor's attempted remake, however, turned out to be a doomed project if there ever was one, and became the only Cukor film ever to be left unfinished.

By the time Ms. Monroe started work on *Something's Got to Give,* her mental health had deteriorated to the point where she was more difficult to work with than ever. For one thing, her failure to show up on the set when she was needed had become a critical problem. "Marilyn was more or less on time when we made *Let's Make Love,*" says Cukor gallantly. "But when we were making *Something's Got to Give,* her preoccupation with her emotional difficulties made it an agony for her to come to the studio at all; and even when she did, she might get sick or fall asleep in her dressing room and fail to report to the set anyhow. I think she knew that she wasn't doing a good job when she did play a scene, and she therefore became more and more terrified of facing the cameras, with the result that she would look for any excuse not to. Her behavior often seemed bullying, as if she were simply being willfully unaccommodating in keeping everyone waiting for her. But she wasn't deliberately heedless, though practically speaking I suppose it came to that. It's sad, but she infuriated just about everyone. And in the end I found that I could no longer reach her."

Cukor had initially planned to shoot the scenes taking place outside of the house of the hero (Dean Martin) on location, but Ms. Monroe's erratic behavior precluded that. "If she were very late coming to the location, we would lose the afternoon sunlight before we finished a scene," Cukor explains. "So it was simpler in the long run to build the exterior of the hero's house in the studio. My home was used as a model for the house, so that the scenic designer could measure its dimensions and then construct the set to scale on the sound stage in a hurry."

In spite of all of Cukor's concessions to Ms. Monroe in order to get the picture made, something had to give, and something did. When the officials at Fox discovered that Cukor had managed to shoot only about one week's worth of usable footage after more than three weeks of filming because of the endless delays Ms. Monroe had caused, they fired her for breach of contract. Lee Remick was briefly considered as a replacement for Ms. Monroe, but the studio finally canceled the picture altogether.

Almost two months to the day after Fox dismissed her, on the night of August 5, 1962, Marilyn Monroe ingested a superlethal concoction of drugs and poison and ended her life. Physicians testified afterwards that she had grown so dependent on drugs as a way of alleviating her severe fits of anxiety and depression, that she had reached the point in her last months where she was utterly incapable of doing any sustained work whatever.

"Once I learned all the facts, I could understand in retrospect that Marilyn had done all she could to cooperate on the film," Cukor comments. "Poor Marilyn was very irritating to work with; but she was a complicated, rather touching creature; and I liked her." It was tragic, he goes on, that the madness that had claimed her mother finally overtook Marilyn Monroe herself. "When she took her life only a few weeks after the picture was shut down, I should have thought that her suicide explained only too clearly that she was too preoccupied with her own private mental anguish to make our movie."

All that remains of *Something's Got to Give* is the footage that was incorporated into a mawkish feature-length documentary called *Marilyn* (1963). For the record, a remake of *My Favorite Wife* was filmed the same year under the title *Move Over, Darling* starring Doris Day and James Garner. The picture was directed by Michael Gordon rather than by Cukor, since at that point Cukor was involved in preparations for one of the best films he ever made.

My Fair Lady (1964)

My Fair Lady marks the peak of Cukor's career in terms of official recognition by the industry. Cukor had been nominated for best director four times before, for *Little Women* (1933), *The Philadelphia Story* (1940), *A Double Life* (1947), and *Born Yesterday* (1950). By the same token, Cukor films had been nominated for best picture four times before, for *Romeo and Juliet* (1936), *The Philadelphia Story*, *Gaslight* (1944), and *Born Yesterday*. For *My Fair Lady* he at long last won the Oscar for best director and the film itself was named best picture of the year.

The movie also brought Cukor the annual award of the Directors' Guild, and it also waltzed off with six other Academy Awards: for Rex Harrison as best actor, Harry Stradling for best color cinematography, Gene Allen and Cecil Beaton for best set design, Beaton again for best costume design, and the Warner Brothers sound department for best sound recording.

Disappointment nonetheless was expressed in some quarters that producer Jack Warner had not chosen Julie Andrews to recreate in the film of *My Fair Lady* the role of Eliza Doolittle that she had already made her own in the original Broadway production. Warner instead chose Audrey Hepburn for the female lead in the movie, because at the time that *My Fair Lady* was being cast Ms. Hepburn was much more of an established box-office draw than Ms. Andrews. Part of the hoopla about Audrey Hepburn being selected over Julie Andrews stemmed from the fact that Marni Nixon dubbed Ms. Hepburn's songs for her on the sound track, whereas Ms. Andrews could have sung them for herself. Yet no one seemed to mind when the ubiquitous Ms. Nixon performed the same chore for Deborah Kerr in *The King and I* (1956) and for Natalie Wood in *West Side Story* (1961).

"Audrey was cast before I came on the picture," says Cukor; "but I was thrilled with the idea of having her play Eliza Doolittle; and I thought she did a lovely job of it. I just got bored to death with all the damned silly fuss about Julie Andrews not getting the part." As for the part of Higgins, Cary Grant—who rejected the role of Norman Maine in Cukor's *A Star Is Born* (1954) because he thought the plot too serious for a musical—was himself passed over for the part of Higgins because, as Cukor explains, "Cary's English was not impeccable enough for him to play a speech expert."

Cecil Beaton, who had costumed the stage production, was engaged in the twin capacity of production designer and costumer for the film at about the same time that Cukor was designated as director. This was Cukor's first color movie without George Hoynigen-Heune as color consultant, but Gene Allen was still with him as art director. As things worked out, Gene Allen was chiefly responsible for the sets while Beaton mostly concentrated on creating the clothes for the movie.

As mentioned before, Cukor had not gotten on well with Beaton when they collaborated on Cukor's last stage production, *The Chalk Garden*, in 1956; and their relationship was not much better this time around. Although the Edwardian outfits Beaton designed for the film were stunning, Cukor described working with him as the only sour note in the whole production. "The differences between me and Cecil Beaton," Cukor notes, "were not on details of interpretation, but on methods of work. He irritated me. I don't think he knows how to work in concert."[3] For example, Beaton would insist on interrupting the rehearsal of a scene right before a take to snap pictures of the cast in costume. This kind of thoughtlessness proved to be a source of infinite annoyance to a director working under the enormous pressures attendant on mounting a complex, multi-million-dollar musical production.

Alan Jay Lerner and Frederick Loewe's musical version of George Bernard Shaw's play *Pygmalion* focuses on the relationship of Henry Higgins, an egotistical speech teacher (Rex Harrison), and Eliza Doolittle, the cockney flower girl whom he transforms into the belle of a society ball on a bet. Initially called *Lady Liza*, the musical finally took its title from the lyrics of an old nursery rhyme: "London bridge is falling down, my fair lady." The title of Shaw's play in turn is a reference to an ancient king of Cyprus who fell in love with the statue of a beautiful maiden which he had carved out of ivory, and which Aphrodite then brought to life in answer to his prayer.

As Shaw conceived the story, says Cukor, Higgins's attempt to fashion Eliza into a refined lady starts out as a battle of wits and only later turns into a romance. "It's the classic relationship of a bullying man and a girl who seems on the surface childlike and malleable, but who possesses a fairly inflexible personality underneath." Eliza is very much the daughter of her father, Alfred P. Doolittle, a dustman (Stanley Holloway); and hence she is wild and untrammeled like him. Her intelligence manifests itself slowly under Higgins's tutoring, and she gradually comes to respect him when she realizes that in the professor she is up against an extremely complicated individual like herself.

Shaw had himself worked on the script for the screen version of *Pygmalion* (1938), codirected by Anthony Asquith and by Leslie Howard, who also played Higgins to Wendy Hiller's Eliza. In the film Shaw allowed the ending of his play, in which the estranged couple do not kiss and make up at the final curtain, to be altered so that Eliza and Henry are clearly reconciled before the final fade-out; and it is this latter ending which Lerner incorporated into both his script for the stage production of *My Fair Lady* and into his screenplay for the film adaptation of the musical. This happy resolution to the plot does not do violence to Shaw's play, as some critics have charged, since the original ending of *Pygmalion* was really ambiguous, and did not close off entirely the possibility of an eventual reunion between Henry and Eliza.

Even though Shaw suggested in the printed epilogue which he appended as an afterthought to the published text of the play that there was a good chance that Eliza might opt for marrying Freddy Eynsford-Hill, a well-bred young gentleman who adores her, the dramatic thrust of the play itself indicates that Eliza would be much more likely to select a mate who possessed a strength of character akin to her own such as Henry Higgins, rather than a vapid, immature fop like Freddy. As for the corresponding likelihood of Higgins's eventual willingness to wed Eliza, the very title Shaw chose for his play in the first place forecasts that Higgins, like his counterpart Pygmalion before him, will finally fall in love with his own creation. Consequently it seems dramatically right that the film version of *My Fair Lady*, like the stage production from which it is derived, should conclude with Henry and Eliza getting back together again.

In the final scene of Cukor's film, Higgins finds himself alone, bemoaning the fact that, in spite of himself, he has undeniably become attached to Eliza. He articulates his feelings in a song called "I've Grown Accustomed to Her Face," which Rex Harrison half sings, half talks, as he does all of his solos in the film, while the lonely Higgins disconsolately mopes his way home on a desolate autumn afternoon. The guarded sentiments expressed in the number are as close to a declaration of love as the reserved professor would ever permit himself to utter. But there is something deeply touching about a man who had fancied himself a confirmed loner having to admit his need and love for another human being.

This scene alone would have qualified Harrison for the Academy Award which he garnered for his portrayal of Higgins, just as his overall performance vindicated once and for all the appropriateness of his first name. Here too the directorial hand of Cukor is evident, as it is throughout the film, guiding Harrison to tone down his original stage performance for the closeness of the camera, and therefore to give a fresh reading of a scene that he had already done more than a thousand times in the theater.

In order to help Harrison to maintain this same air of spontaneity in delivering his solo numbers in the film, Cukor had him record them directly onto the sound track while the number was actually being filmed, as opposed to prerecording them and using the playbacks during shooting. This approach worked particularly well in the case of "I've Grown Accustomed to Her Face," since it enabled Harrison to bring to his delivery of the song a degree of pathos when he shot the scene that would not have been possible had he been merely miming the lyrics to a prerecorded rendition of the number done beforehand.

In rethinking the stage musical for the screen, Cukor came up with some fine visual symbols to underline the meaning of a scene or point up a character's personality. While maintaining his knightly vigil underneath Eliza's window, the weak, passive Freddy sings a worshipful hymn to her entitled "On the Street Where You Live." As he finishes the song, his silhouette sinks into the shadows around him and virtually disappears, indicating how insubstantial a creature he really is.

Earlier in the movie, when Eliza visits Higgins for the first time, he has his housekeeper and maids strongarm the scruffy, unkempt girl upstairs for a long-overdue bath. The steam from the hot tub billows up and blots her out from view, as if the old Eliza has vanished, to be replaced by the clean-cut young woman who shortly emerges from the bathroom in crisp new clothes, ready to be remodeled into the fair lady that Higgins plans to make of her.

In transferring *My Fair Lady* to the screen Cukor left his unmistakable stamp on every aspect of the production, as Charles Higham testifies in his history of American cinema. "Cukor's personality is much in evidence, dominating even that of Cecil Beaton," whose

designs "express no less striking intelligence and flair." In the relaxed
playing of Rex Harrison and Audrey Hepburn, "in the subtly unobtrusive flow of camerawork and editing, in the marshalling of the
supporting cast into agreeable patterns within the frame, Cukor's
skill shows an undimmed luster."[4]

The Blue Bird (1976)

Just about any musical Cukor made after the triumph of *My Fair
Lady* would, I suppose, be something of an anticlimax; and, truth to
tell, Cukor's most recent musical, *The Blue Bird*, is not in the same
league with the earlier work. In fairness, however, one must record
that Cukor encountered obstacles in making *The Blue Bird* that
would have daunted directors many years his junior. In actual fact a
couple of younger filmmakers approached by Fox to direct the picture did decline to take on this imposing project when they considered the possibility of spending almost a year in Russia making a
large-scale movie with a bilingual Russian-American cast and crew,
not to mention coping with such formidable American superstars as
Elizabeth Taylor, Ava Gardner, and Jane Fonda.

"The idea of a co-production between Russia and the United States
had been in the air for more than six years," Cukor recalls. "Everyone
wanted something fairly non-political that would be meaningful to
audiences in both our countries." *The Blue Bird*, a musical fantasy by
Nobel-prizewinning playwright Maurice Maeterlinck, seemed the
most likely candidate for the coproduction. "I had seen the play when
I was very young," Cukor continues, "and read it again when I was
invited to direct the picture. I found it still fresh and touching, and
agreed to do it."

Cukor departed for Leningrad to begin preparations for the production in October 1974; principal photography commenced in
January 1975 and finished the following autumn. In addition to the
inevitable problems inherent in a complicated coproduction of this
kind, the unexpected snags which confronted Cukor from time to
time included the periodic illnesses which plagued the English-
speaking members of the unit, who found it hard to become accustomed to both the Russian winter and the Russian diet. The Russians'
technical equipment also took some getting used to, since it was not
up to American standards. "I'm working on equipment that is prehis-
toric," an American editor complained to journalist Rex Reed when
the latter visited the studio. "You won't believe it, but this picture is

being edited on a 1921 moviola like the one Eisenstein used on *Potemkin*."[5]

On his return to America after completing the film, Cukor made some observations of his own about working conditions in the Russian film industry. "I like the Russians enormously," he began; "but I found it harrowing that they were not very well organized." The advance preparations for shooting were not thoroughly made before Cukor arrived in Leningrad, and once he began filming he found that the Russian technicians were neither as accomplished nor as efficient as those he had brought with him. Yet somehow the movie got made.

Cukor's film of *The Blue Bird* is a remake, with a new original musical score, of the film directed in 1939 by Walter Lang as a vehicle for Shirley Temple, intended at the time to be Fox's answer to MGM's *Wizard of Oz;* and the plot of Cukor's version follows the earlier film fairly closely. It is the tale of a young brother (Todd Lookinland) and sister (Patsy Kensit) who leave home in the company of their cat (Cicely Tyson) and dog (George Cole) to find the blue bird of happiness.

After visiting the dark domain of Night (Jane Fonda), the frivolous encampment of Luxury (Ava Gardner), and other strange places, the children return home only to find the blue bird of happiness where it has always been—in their own backyard. Cured of their wish to immerse themselves in a world of fantasy, they are happy to be welcomed back into the world of reality by their loving mother (Elizabeth Taylor, who by turns also plays the Spirit of Maternal Love, Light, and a witch in the course of the movie). Even this brief synopsis of the movie makes it evident that *The Blue Bird* brought Cukor back once again to familiar thematic territory, dealing as it does with the interplay of fantasy and reality.

A highlight of the bizarre junket of the two children and their companions to various unearthly places is their visit to the kingdom of the children waiting to be born, presided over by Robert Morley as Father Time, whose sprightly patter song about the manner in which Time rules us all amounts to a nifty music-hall turn. Another charming set piece is the ballet duet of Fire (Eugene Tscherbakov), dressed in flashy orange tights, and Water (Valentina Ganibalova), wearing a cool white outfit. Their dance is climaxed by Fire and Water embracing and accordingly evaporating into a cloud of steam.

Cukor sought as much as possible to be faithful to the style and spirit of his literary source. "I toned down the sentimental aspects of the story as much as I could," he says; "but, as I mentioned with

Cukor in separate poses with his four female stars in The Blue Bird *(1976): (clockwise from top left) Elizabeth Taylor, Jane Fonda, Cicely Tyson and Ava Gardner.*

reference to filming *David Copperfield* [1935], you can't change the original work which you are filming in any major fashion without running the risk of removing some of its strengths along with its weaknesses. In any event, I think *The Blue Bird* holds up very well, though it was written many years ago, since the human values at its core can never go out of date."

Cukor's *Blue Bird* is much more animated and vigorous than the stolid 1939 version, in which the actors tended to strike attitudes as if they were appearing in a school pageant. Yet there are some dull, sentimental stretches in the 1976 remake, as when the boy and girl visit their dead grandparents, into which perhaps no director could have breathed much vitality. In any case, the new version of *The Blue Bird* never took flight at the box office, though it found a much wider audience when it was telecast for the first time in the summer of 1980.

In assessing Cukor's musicals one can say that, although they are not of equal merit, each of them reflects the unerring taste and creative imagination of the man who directed them all. As Pauline Kael once wrote in this regard, "I applaud the commercial heroism of a director who can steer a huge production" while keeping his sanity, perspective, and decent human feelings beautifully intact.[6] Surely these words can be as appropriately applied to George Cukor as to any other maker of movie musicals.

7

Epilogue:
More Than an Entertainer

"HOLLYWOOD'S LIKE EGYPT, FULL OF CRUMBLED PYRAMIDS. It will just keep crumbling until finally the wind blows the last studio prop across the sand," David O. Selznick once remarked. "There might have been good movies if there had been no movie industry. Hollywood might have become the center of a new human expression if it hadn't been grabbed by a little group of bookkeepers and turned into a junk industry."[1]

These are bitter words indeed to come from the producer with whom Cukor labored on significant films like *Dinner at Eight* (1933) and *David Copperfield* (1935), not to mention *Gone With the Wind* (1939). Nevertheless, Selznick's statement vividly crystallizes the problem that has vexed creative movie makers ever since motion pictures became big business: the problem of trying to make motion pictures that are personal, unified works of art which a director can truly call his own, despite the fact that he is working in a large, complex commercial industry.

To establish that Cukor has largely succeeded in this hazardous enterprise throughout his long career, one need only examine his impressive filmography. Referring to Cukor, Andrew Sarris has pointed out that, when a director has consistently dished up tasteful entertainment of a high order for half a century, it is clear that he is much more than a mere entertainer; "he is a genuine artist."[2]

In fact, it could be said that Cukor is the prototype of the ideal Hollywood director, for he has over the years weathered the changes in public taste and the pressures of the studio system without compromising his style, his taste, or his ethical standards. Furthermore, because he is a skilled craftman who recognizes that a good film is the product of many talents, he has therefore been able to work successfully with all sorts of collaborators, as I saw firsthand when I visited

Cukor directing Candice Bergen in Rich and Famous *(1981), which he made at the age of 81.*

the set of *Rich and Famous* recently, and at the same time always add a personal touch to the wide variety of films he has directed.

All of Cukor's individual films have become part of the total canon of his work, and he has informed each of them with his affectionately critical view of humanity. In movie after movie he has sought to prod the mass audience to reconsider their cherished illusions in order to gain fresh insights into the common problems that confront us all. Cukor, as I said earlier, may sympathize with the need that his characters on occasion feel to take refuge in the world of romantic illusion. But his films nevertheless remain firmly rooted in, and committed to, the workaday world of everyday reality with which his characters must sooner or later come to terms.

Anyone who has survived the Hollywood factory system as long as Cukor has will inevitably have experienced his share of both ups and downs. Among the reversals he has suffered, in addition to being replaced as director of *One Hour with You* (1932) and of *Gone With the Wind,* was having *Desire Me* (1947) taken away from him after he finished it and partially reshot by two other directors. The story line of *Desire Me* is really a turnabout of the plot of another ill-fated Cukor project, the unfinished *Something's Got to Give* (1962), dealing as it does with a young woman (Greer Garson) who falls in love with another man after her husband (Robert Mitchum) is presumed dead, only to have him unexpectedly reappear on the scene.

Cukor shot the movie under the title *Sacred and Profane* from a muddled screenplay. Then the studio had the script reworked by other writers with the new title of *Desire Me,* and brought in Jack Conway and Mervyn LeRoy to film the new scenes. "Whenever a picture doesn't turn out, the studio always assumes that it is the director's fault," Cukor explains. "I was put off *Desire Me* because the front office blamed everything on me." The new version of the film was not satisfactory either, however; and neither Cukor nor his two replacements wanted any screen credit for directing the film. "And so *Desire Me* became the only major Hollywood feature to be released in America without a directorial credit," Cukor concludes, "although I believe my name appeared as director on the prints of the film circulated in England anyway, in spite of the fact that I had totally disowned the picture."

Cukor's old friend Fanny Brice used to say, "If you stay in the card game long enough, sooner or later the deal comes round to you." Only a few years after the *Desire Me* fiasco, David Selznick, who had fired Cukor from *Gone With the Wind* back in 1939, asked Cukor to replace Mervyn LeRoy, one of the directors who had taken over *Desire Me*, as the director of the remake of *Little Women* (1949), though Cukor declined to do so for the reasons given in Chapter 3. Still later, Cukor was brought in by MGM to finish the Esther Williams musical *Million Dollar Mermaid* (1952) when LeRoy was cashiered near the end of shooting. Cukor consoled LeRoy on the latter occasion by saying, "I was put off *Gone With the Wind*, maybe the biggest movie ever made, and I'm still here to tell the tale; so don't despair. You must have faith in yourself and keep going."

Among the other pictures for which Cukor has assumed direction for one reason or another is a picture called *Song Without End* (1960). When its director, Charles Vidor, died after a month of shooting, Cukor completed this film about Franz Liszt (Dirk Bogarde). But he asked that directorial credit go solely to Vidor, who had done a significant portion of the film before Cukor took over. The producer honored Cukor's request, but he sneaked a special word of thanks to Cukor into the credits.

Rich and Famous (1981)

When an actors' strike halted production on MGM's *Rich and Famous* for more than two months, the original director, Robert Mulligan, withdrew because of the encroachment of other commitments. He suggested Cukor as his replacement because, as he observed, *Rich and Famous* is the kind of stylish comedy of manners that Cukor has excelled in making for years. When shooting was resumed on November 10, 1980, George Cukor was in fact at the helm, embarking on his fiftieth film as a director in just about as many years. Asked how he felt about stepping in for Mulligan, the eighty-one-year-old filmmaker replied serenely, no doubt thinking of movies like *Desire Me* and *Million Dollar Mermaid*, "I've replaced other directors and other directors have replaced me. But, you know, if I wasn't sure that I was still able and ready to direct a picture, I wouldn't have agreed to do it."

Mulligan had only completed one week of shooting when production was stopped by the actors' walkout, and Cukor reshot most of that when he took over the directorship of the film. Though Cukor is in good health, he made one or two reluctant concessions to his years during shooting, such as snatching a quick nap during the lunch break; but otherwise he carried on business as usual exactly as he has always done.

Based loosely on the play *Old Acquaintance* by John Van Druten, *Rich and Famous* is a streamlined, contemporary version of the story, which therefore differs greatly from Vincent Sherman's 1943 film *Old Acquaintance*, derived from the same play. The present film has Jacqueline Bisset and Candice Bergen standing in for Bette Davis and Miriam Hopkins, the costars of the earlier movie, as Liz and Merry, two college coeds who become bitter rivals in both their personal and professional lives as the years go on. The project was initiated by producer William Allyn, who saw the first film version on the late show and engaged screen writer Gerald Ayres to write a fresh adaptation of the story for the 1980s, using Van Druten's play as his point of departure. He then went on to assemble a distinguished group of artists to work on the film, including French composer George Delerue, who won an Oscar in 1980 for his music for *A Little Romance*, to write the score. (*Old Acquaintance* may now be forgot.)

When I visited the set of *Rich and Famous* near the end of the shooting period, Cukor remarked that he was particularly glad to be filming at MGM, a studio where he had made so many films. He thought Metro had not changed much since the days when he worked there regularly. "Coming back after some years away," he said, "I noticed that, despite the fact that the personnel is different (there is only one sour old secretary still around from my time there), the high standards set by L. B. Mayer and the others of his time have remained intact. The tradition of excellence and craftsmanship seems somehow buried in the walls of this place, and has never left it."

He introduced me to, among others, art director Fred Harpman, whom he had found especially helpful in working out the visual composition of various shots, in much the same way that Gene Allen and others had been in years gone by. "It's very rare in my twenty-five years in the picture business," said Harpman, "to find a director of George Cukor's stature who understands the collaborative nature of making movies to the degree that he does. He is always ready to listen to fresh ideas from myself, the cameraman, or anyone else before he makes his final decision on how a scene should look. It's an enormous privilege to work with a man who encourages the people around him to give free reign to their own artistic ingenuity."

When Cukor first saw the set for the Greenwich Village apartment of Liz (Jacqueline Bisset), he thought it a trifle too funky and slovenly for a serious writer like Liz, and conferred with Harpman on ways of touching up the set a bit. "It looked too much like a conventional movie set," Cukor explained, "because it was not sufficiently tailored to the personality of Liz, who is, after all, a woman of taste and intelligence. So Fred and I talked about ways of making the apartment reflect a bit more of the individual character of the person living there, as every set should." Then Harpman went ahead and redressed the set, and gave Cukor just what he wanted, while adding some nice details of his own.

At this point in the shooting schedule Cukor is working on a delicate scene, late in the picture, which takes place in the swank New York apartment of Merry, a successful commercial novelist (Candice Bergen), in which Merry and Liz share a moment of truth. "It's a thoughtful, subtle scene," says Cukor, "one which the actors can dig into." Jacqueline Bisset asks Cukor if she should cry during the scene, and is told by the director to fight back her tears at first, and then finally let them break through. "It is more moving and effective if a character doesn't weep too soon in a scene," he notes between takes. "If an actor cries too easily on the screen, the audience probably won't cry at all."

The shot at hand is a complicated one in which the action starts at the far end of the large living-room set and then moves progressively toward the camera at the other end of the room, where there is an important interchange of dialogue. "Print that," Cukor says after an especially good take. "But let's do it one more time at a faster clip, just for the hell of it." Then, to make sure that everyone is in place, he calls out in a voice that is at once courteous and commanding, "Can we go now, ladies and gentlemen!" while he slaps his rolled-up script against his leg as if it were a riding crop. He is king of the mountain, but the only throne he has ever coveted is the director's chair in which he now settles down to watch another take. "Print that one, too; that was fine," he says with satisfaction. "Thank you, ladies and gentlemen."

While the crew is setting up the next shot, Cukor tells me that, although he is glad to be back at MGM, it was really the quality of the screenplay that drew him to direct *Rich and Famous*. "I still find a witty, intelligent script irresistible," he says. "And I'm sticking right to the text as always. I don't come in each day with new lines of my own scribbled on the back of an envelope." Listening to the actors speak their lines, one can understand why Cukor was attracted by the screenplay's clever, biting dialogue. Referring to the fact that Liz is a respected writer who has never had a bestseller, Merry comments in a rare moment of generous candor that, instead of being rich and famous like herself, Liz is "only famous—which is harder to do."

But the script has visual as well as verbal gems for Cukor to mine. One visual symbol that pervades the film is the teddy bear which Liz and Merry have both cherished since they were college roommates. In a fit of mutual bitchiness during a climactic quarrel near the end of the movie, each claims the bear as her own; and they literally tear the stuffing out of this treasured souvenir of their youth so that neither of them can keep it, thereby destroying the last vestige of the happy college days they had shared together.

In the final sequence of the film they are once more reconciled to each other as they spend New Year's Eve alone together. Appropriately enough, they toast the New Year with champagne that has gone flat, sadly symbolic of the way their personal lives have likewise gone stale. They are two lonely, abandoned females, both well into their thirties, aware that all that is left of their broken lives is their relationship with each other: a lovely, elegiac note on which to conclude the film.

Directing *Rich and Famous* merited Cukor the distinction of being very likely the oldest filmmaker ever to direct a major motion picture, and likewise marked him as enjoying the longest continuous career in movies and TV of any director ever. As we concluded our conversation about the film, Cukor joked that, in watching a man of his age make a movie, I am witnessing "the twilight of the gods." I responded that, in pursuing his art into his eighties, Cukor joins the ranks of Verdi and Vaughan Williams, who did the same; not bad company to be in.

As I watched Cukor direct *Rich and Famous*, it was obvious to me that he has lost none of the enthusiasm for the movie business which he brought with him to Hollywood in 1929. "I look upon every picture that I make as the first one I've ever done—and the last," he once reflected to me. "I love each film I have directed, and I try to make each one as good as I possibly can. Mind you, making movies is no bed of roses. Every day isn't Christmas. It's been a hard life, but also a joyous one." Cukor has received his share of accolades, including most recently the prestigious D. W. Griffith Award from the Directors Guild of America in 1981, which has only been awarded thirteen times since its inception in 1953.

No doubt some of the satisfaction which Cukor derives from his career is grounded in the fact that few directors have commanded such a large portion of the mass audience. "His movies," Richard Schickel has written, "can be appreciated—no, liked—at one level or another by just about everyone."[3]

Hence Cukor's films, even the earliest of them, continue to turn up on TV and at revival houses across the country, and to circulate in 16 mm to the educational market. As Andrew Sarris has remarked, some films age; others date. Cukor's films clearly belong to the first category.

Perhaps the most touching compliment Cukor has received recently came from a young director named Walter Hill (*Hard Times*), who admires the work of his now venerable predecessor very much. "I couldn't make a George Cukor movie," said Hill. "I don't know how. I wish I could. I think they're great, and we probably need films like that these days."[4]

Indeed we do.

Notes and References

Chapter One

1. David O. Selznick, *Memo from David O. Selznick*, ed. Rudy Behlmer (New York, 1973), p. 45.
2. Letter to Gene Phillips, June 16, 1980.
3. Quoted in Romano V. Tozzi, "George Cukor," *Films in Review*, February 19, 1958, p. 54.

Chapter Two

1. Andrew Sarris, *The American Cinema* (New York: Dutton, 1968), pp. 89–90.
2. Richard Griffith and Arthur Mayer, *The Movies*, rev. ed. (New York: Simon and Schuster, 1970), p. 279.
3. Jeffrey Richards, *"Our Betters,"* *Focus on Film*, Spring 1979, p. 42.
4. John Russell Taylor, ed., *Graham Greene on Film* (New York: Simon and Schuster, 1972), p. 11.
5. Quoted in Gavin Lambert, *On Cukor* (New York, 1973), p. 104.
6. Andrew Sarris, "Two or Three Things I Know About *Gaslight*," *Film Comment* 12 (May–June 1976):24.
7. Selznick, p. 396.
8. Charles Higham, "The Forties," in Peter Cowie, ed., *Hollywood: 1920–70* (New York: Barnes, 1977), p. 124; *The Art of the American Film* (Garden City, N.Y.: Doubleday, 1974), p. 185.
9. James Agee, *Agee on Film* (New York: Grosset and Dunlop, 1969), 1:135.
10. Quoted in "Party," *People*, April 30, 1978, p. 53.
11. Pauline Kael, *Going Steady* (New York: Bantam Books, 1971), pp. 284–85.

Chapter Three

1. Selznick, p. 73.
2. Letter to Gene Phillips, November 12, 1973.

3.   From a taped dialogue between Cukor and Katharine Hepburn in Cukor's personal archive, dated summer 1969. Unless specifically noted otherwise, any quotations from Hepburn in this book are from this source.

4.   Gary Carey, *Cukor and Company* (New York, 1971), p. 42.

5.   George Cukor, "The Director," in *Hollywood Directors: 1914–40*, ed. Richard Koszarski (New York, 1976), p. 330.

6.   Allen Estrin, *The Hollywood Professionals* (New York, 1980), 6:122.

7.   Carey, p. 76.

8.   Quoted in Larry Swindell, *Spencer Tracy* (New York: New American Library, 1971), p. 164.

9.   Quoted in John Baxter, *Sixty Years of Hollywood* (New York: Barnes, 1973), p. 137.

10.   Quoted in Swindell, p. 196.

11.   Pauline Kael, *Kiss, Kiss, Bang, Bang* (New York: Bantam Books, 1969), p. 414.

12.   Quoted in Richard Schickel, *The Men Who Made the Movies* (New York, 1975), p. 177.

13.   Carey, p. 166.

14.   Quoted in Rex Reed, *Conversations in the Raw* (New York: World, 1969), p. 28.

15.   Douglas McVay, "In Praise of Jean Simmons," *Focus on Film*, Summer 1969, p. 38.

16.   Letter to Gene Phillips, July 17, 1974.

17.   Carlos Clemens, *George Cukor* (London, 1976), p. 126.

18.   Katharine Hepburn, "So Just Keep a-Goin'—You Can Win," *TV Guide*, January 27, 1979, p. 5.

19.   Quoted in Benedict Nightingale, "After Making Nine Films Together, Hepburn Can Practically Direct Cukor," *New York Times*, January 28, 1979, 2:1,29.

20.   Letter to Gene Phillips, January 15, 1979.

21.   "Hepburn Shines in Revival," *Time*, January 29, 1979, p. 66.

22.   "So Just Keep a-Goin'," p. 5.

23.   Quoted in "Party," *People*, April 30, 1978, p. 53.

Chapter Four

1.   Kael, *Kiss, Kiss, Bang, Bang*, p. 300.

2.   Bosley Crowther, *The Great Films: Fifty Golden Years of Motion Pictures* (New York: Putnam, 1967), p. 120.

3.   Letter to Gene Phillips, August 13, 1980.

4.   Quoted in Lawrence J. Quirk, *The Films of Robert Taylor* (Secaucus, N.J.: Citadel Press, 1979), p. 56.

5.   Stephen Harvey, *Joan Crawford* (New York: Pyramid, 1975), p. 82.

6. Cukor, "The Director," in *Hollywood Directors: 1914–40*, p. 329.

7. Quoted in "Party," *People*, April 30, 1978, p. 53.

8. Harvey, p. 84.

9. Joan Crawford, with Jane Kesner Ardmore, *A Portrait of Joan* (Garden City, N.Y.: Doubleday, 1962), pp. 126–27.

10. Quoted in *Directors at Work: Interviews with American Film Makers*, ed. Bernard R. Kantor, Irwin R. Blacker, and Anne Kramer (New York, 1970), p. 80.

11. Gordon Gow, "The Fifties," in Peter Cowie, ed., *Hollywood: 1920–70* (New York: Barnes, 1977), p. 214.

12. Quoted in Rex Reed, *Travolta to Keaton* (New York: William Morrow, 1979), p. 60.

13. Richard Roud, "George Cukor," in *A Special Gala in Honor of George Cukor* (New York: Lincoln Center of the Performing Arts, 1978), p. 18.

14. Joseph McBride, "Film Favorites: *What Price Hollywood?*," *Film Comment* 9 (May 1973):64.

15. Letter to Gene Phillips, July 28, 1980.

16. Quoted in "Whirlwind Tour," *Time*, February 12, 1973, p. 57.

Chapter Five

1. Selznick, p. 91.

2. Quoted in Richard Schickel, *The Men Who Made the Movies* (New York, 1975), p. 178.

3. Andre Sennwald, "*David Copperfield*," *New York Times*, January 19, 1935, p. 8.

4. Selznick, p. 225.

5. Quoted in Charles Higham, *Hollywood Cameramen: Sources of Light* (Bloomington: Indiana University Press, 1970), p. 46.

6. Cf. Gavin Lambert, *GWTW: The Making of Gone With the Wind* (Boston: Little, Brown, 1973), p. 118.

7. Selznick, p. 288.

8. Quoted in Clarens, *George Cukor*, p. 180.

9. Letter to Gene Phillips, January 20, 1971.

10. Letters to Gene Phillips, June 4, 1974; March 26, 1980.

11. Letter to Gene Phillips, March 27, 1972.

12. Jay Cocks, "Whirlwind Tour," *Time*, February 12, 1973.

Chapter Six

1. Joseph McBride, "Film Favorites: *What Price Hollywood?*," *Film Comment* 9 (May 1973):64.

2. Estrin, 6:104.

3. Quoted in Charles Higham and Joel Greenberg, *The Celluloid Muse: Hollywood Directors Speak* (New York, 1969), pp. 75–76; cf. Cecil

Beaton, *Self Portrait with Friends: The Selected Diaries, 1926–74*, ed. Richard Buckle (New York: Times Books, 1979), pp. 366–67.

    4.   Higham, *The Art of the American Film*, p. 187.

    5.   Quoted in Rex Reed, *Valentines and Vitriol* (New York, 1978), p. 44.

    6.   Kael, *Going Steady*, p. 251.

Chapter Seven

    1.   Quoted in Ben Hecht, "Enter the Movies," in *Film: An Anthology*, ed. Daniel Talbot (Berkeley: University of California Press, 1966), p. 258.

    2.   Sarris, *The American Cinema* pp. 89–90.

    3.   Schickel, p. 164.

    4.   Quoted in Michael Greco, "Hard Riding," *Film Comment* 15 (May–June 1980):14.

Selected Bibliography

1. Books

Carey, Gary. *Cukor and Company: The Films of George Cukor and His Collaborators*. New York: The Museum of Modern Art, 1971. A well-researched study of all of Cukor's films up to *Justine*. The author's mercurial judgments of some of Cukor's films, however, lessen the volume's value.

Clarens, Carlos. *George Cukor*. London: Secker and Warburg, 1976. The Cukor interview material interspersed throughout the filmography at the back of the book is sometimes of more interest than what the author has to say up front, since he at times gets unduly involved in side issues of, e.g., a sociological or theological nature which he lacks the space to develop adequately.

Film Society of Lincoln Center, The. *A Special Gala in Honor of George Cukor*. New York: Lincoln Center for the Performing Arts, 1978. This souvenir program for the tribute to Cukor on April 30, 1978 (which the director calls his belated bar mitzvah in the cinema!), is highlighted by Richard Roud's penetrating assessment of Cukor's contribution to film art.

Gordon, Ruth, and Kanin, Garson. *Adam's Rib*. The MGM Library of Film Scripts. New York: Viking Press, 1972. The Kanins' brilliant screenplay for the Cukor comedy is presented here with footnotes that detail any alterations made in the script during shooting.

Lambert, Gavin. *On Cukor*. New York: Capricorn Books, 1973. Ranks with François Truffaut's *Hitchcock* as one of the finest book-length interviews with a director ever published. A witty, incisive study of a filmmaker by a very knowledgeable writer.

My Fair Lady. New York: Alsid Distributors, 1964. A useful brochure about the making of the film, sumptuously illustrated in color, which profiles the major cast and production staff members as well as the director.

184 GEORGE CUKOR

Selznick, David O. *Memo from: David O. Selznick*. Edited by Rudy Behlmer. New York: Avon Books, 1973. A fascinating collection of primary source material which includes many interesting items about the Cukor films which Selznick produced, though one must beware of Selznick's hyperbolic and self-aggrandizing writing style.

2. Parts of Books

Beaton, Cecil. *Self Portrait with Friends: The Selected Diaries, 1926–74*. Edited by Richard Buckle. New York: Times Books, 1979, pp. 355–68. These passages from Beaton's diaries cover the filming of *My Fair Lady* and comment on his uneasy working relationship with Cukor, dealt with in the treatment of the film in this book.

Cukor, George. "The Director." In Richard Koszarski, ed. *Hollywood Directors: 1914–40*. New York: Oxford University Press, 1976, pp. 322–31. Although originally published in 1938, this essay by Cukor is still a substantially accurate presentation of his views on his craft, particularly emphasizing the collaborative nature of filmmaking.

Estrin, Allen. *The Hollywood Professionals*. Vol. 6. New York: Barnes, 1980. The author has some perceptive things to say, but devotes a disproportionate amount of space to analyzing Cukor's movies in terms of their implications for the feminist movement.

Higham, Charles, and Greenberg, Joel. *The Celluloid Muse: Hollywood Directors Speak*. New York: New American Library, 1972. The candid and informative interview with Cukor in this book contains data not to be found anywhere else about some of his lesser-known films and unrealized projects.

Kantor, Bernard R.; Blacker, Irwin R.; and Kramer, Anne. *Directors at Work: Interviews with American Filmmakers*. New York: Funk and Wagnalls, 1970. Significantly, the authors preface their interview with Cukor by remarking that he was in many ways the most difficult director to interview. That is because the questions put to him are too often imprecise or irrelevant (e.g., "Would Cukor have directed *Georgy Girl*?").

Overstreet, Richard. "George Cukor." In Andrew Sarris, ed. *Interviews with Film Directors*. New York: Avon Books, 1969, pp. 92–126. A long, wide-ranging interview that is especially helpful in accenting some of the technical problems Cukor has encountered in making movies, such as filming in wide screen and color.

Reed, Rex. *Valentines and Vitriol*. New York: Dell, 1977. Contains a bitingly satirical account of Cukor's production problems while shooting *The Blue Bird* (1976) in Russia. For a more balanced view of the making of the film, cf. John Russell Taylor, "George Cukor's *Blue Bird*," *The Times* (London), September 18, 1975.

Schickel, Richard. *The Men Who Made the Movies.* New York: Atheneum, 1975. The full transcript of the interview, which Schickel filmed for the Cukor segment of his TV mini-series of the same title, is included in this book. The material is conveniently arranged under headings, so that one can easily find Cukor's thoughts on any subject covered in the interview.

3. Articles

Gray, Beverly. "A Conversation with George Cukor." *Performing Arts,* August 1980, pp. 12–18. A delightful interview article which gives Cukor's reflections on general topics such as the studio system and current cinematic trends.

Hepburn, Katharine. "So Just Keep A-Goin'—You Can Win." *TV Guide,* January 27, 1979, pp. 4–11. A firsthand memoir about filming the television movie of *The Corn Is Green* (1979) on location in Wales, which also sums up the long professional relationship of Cukor and Hepburn. (Cf. her article, "Get a Tough Director," *Panorama,* March 1981, pp. 58–61, 77.)

Powers, James. "Dialogue on Film: George Cukor." *American Film* 3 (February 1978):33–48. The edited transcript of a seminar which Cukor gave for advanced film students under the auspices of the American Film Institute in which the director is particularly frank about the problems of the film artist who is working in an industry.

Tozzi, Romano V. "George Cukor." *Films in Review,* February 1958, pp. 53–64. A somewhat superficial but fact-filled essay covering Cukor's career up to *Bhowani Junction,* which begins with an excellent account of his youth and work in the theater.

4. Unpublished Material

Cukor, George. Typed letters signed to Gene Phillips, dated from Hollywood, 1971–81. Cukor's correspondence over this period contains references to the making of his films of the 1970s, as well as to several of his previous pictures.

Greene, Graham. Typed letters signed to Gene Phillips, dated from France, March 27, 1972; June 4, 1974; and March 26, 1980. Greene discusses Cukor's film adaptation of his novel *Travels with My Aunt* (1972) both before and after the movie was made.

Zinnemann, Fred. Typed letter signed to Gene Phillips, dated from London, June 16, 1980. Zinnemann recalls working as an extra in *All Quiet on the Western Front* (1930), on which Cukor was dialogue director, and serving as an assistant to Cukor on *Camille* (1936). "Since then we have occasionally met socially on very friendly terms," Zinnemann concludes; "and, needless to say, I have enormous respect for George and for his work."

Filmography

1. Feature Films
Cukor served as dialogue director on *River of Romance* (Paramount, 1929) and on *All Quiet on the Western Front* (Universal, 1930, uncredited). He was also listed as dialogue director on *One Hour with You* (Paramount, 1932), a portion of which he directed on his own.

Cukor codirected the following features:

GRUMPY (Paramount, 1930)
Codirector: Cyril Gardner
Cast: Cyril Maude (Grumpy Bullivant), Paul Lukas (Berci)
16 mm Rental: Clem Williams

THE VIRTUOUS SIN (Paramount, 1930—British title, CAST IRON)
Codirector: Louis Gasnier
Cast: Walter Huston (General Gregori Platoff), Kay Francis (Maria Ivanova)
16 mm Rental: Clem Williams

THE ROYAL FAMILY OF BROADWAY (Paramount, 1930)
Codirector: Cyril Gardner
Cast: Fredric March (Tony Cavendish), Ina Claire (Julia Cavendish)
16 mm Rental: Clem Williams

Cukor directed the following features:

TARNISHED LADY (Paramount, 1931)
Producer: Walter Wanger
Script: Donald Ogden Stewart. Based on his story *New York Lady*

Director of Photography: Larry Williams
Editor: Barney Rogan
Cast: Tallulah Bankhead (Nancy Courtney), Clive Brook (Norman Cravath),
Alexander Kirkland (DeWitt Taylor), Osgood Perkins (Ben Sterner)
Running Time: 80 minutes
Premiere: April 1931, New York
16 mm Rental: Clem Williams

GIRLS ABOUT TOWN (Paramount, 1931)
Script: Raymond Griffith, Brian Marlow. Based on a story by Zoë Akins
Director of Photography: Ernest Haller
Cast: Kay Francis (Wanda Howard), Joel McCrea (Jim Baker), Lilyan
Tashman (Marie Bailey), Eugene Pallette (Benjamin Thomas)
Running Time: 66 minutes
Premiere: October 1931, New York
16 mm Rental: Clem Williams

WHAT PRICE HOLLYWOOD? (RKO, 1932)
Producer: David O. Selznick
Associate Producer: Pandro S. Berman
Script: Gene Fowler, Rowland Brown. Based on a story by Adela Rogers St.
Johns
Director of Photography: Charles Rosher
Editor: Jack Kitchin
Music: Max Steiner
Cast: Constance Bennett (Mary Evans), Lowell Sherman (Maximilian
Carey), Neil Hamilton (Lonny Borden), Gregory Ratoff (Julius Saxe)
Running Time: 88 minutes
Premiere: June 1932, New York
16 mm Rental: Films, Inc. Also available on videocassette

A BILL OF DIVORCEMENT (RKO, 1932)
Producer: David O. Selznick
Script: Howard Estabrook, Harry Wagstaff Gribble. Based on the play by
Clemence Dane
Director of Photography: Sid Hickox
Editor: Arthur Roberts
Set Designer: Carroll Clark
Costumes: Josette De Lima
Music: Max Steiner
Cast: John Barrymore (Hilary), Billie Burke (Margaret), Katharine Hepburn
(Sydney), David Manners (Kit), Henry Stephenson (Dr. Alliot)

Running Time: 70 minutes
Premiere: September 1932, New York
16 mm Rental: Audio-Brandon

ROCKABYE (RKO, 1932)
Script: Jane Murfin, Kubec Glasmon. Based on the play by Lucia Bronder
Director of Photography: Charles Rosher
Uncredited Director: George Fitzmaurice (replaced by Cukor)
Editor: George Hively
Music: Max Steiner
Cast: Constance Bennett (Judy Carrol), Paul Lukas (De Sola), Joel McCrea (Jake Pell), Jobyna Howland (Snooks), Walter Pidgeon (Commissioner Howard)
Running Time: 71 minutes
Premiere: November 1932, New York
16 mm Rental: Films Inc.

OUR BETTERS (RKO, 1933)
Executive Producer: David O. Selznick
Script: Jane Murfin, Harry Wagstaff Gribble. Based on the play by W. Somerset Maugham
Director of Photography: Charles Rosher
Editor: Jack Kitchin
Music: Max Steiner
Art Directors: Van Nest Polglase and Hobe Erwin
Cast: Constance Bennett (Lady Pearl Grayston), Gilbert Roland (Peppi D'Costa), Alan Mowbray (Lord George Grayston), Violet Kemble-Cooper (Duchess)
Running Time: 72 minutes
Premiere: March 1933, New York
16 mm Rental: Films Inc.

DINNER AT EIGHT (MGM, 1933)
Executive Producer: David O. Selznick
Script: Herman J. Mankiewicz, Frances Marion, Donald Ogden Stewart. Based on the play by Edna Ferber and George S. Kaufman
Director of Photography: William Daniels
Editor: Ben Lewis
Set Designers: Hobe Erwin, Fred Hope
Costumes: Adrian
Music: William Axt
Cast: Marie Dressler (Carlotta Vance), John Barrymore (Larry Renault),

Wallace Beery (Dan Packard), Jean Harlow (Kitty Packard), Lionel
Barrymore (Oliver Jordan), Lee Tracy (Max Kane), Edmund Lowe (Dr.
Wayne Talbot), Billie Burke (Mrs. Oliver Jordan)
Running Time: 110 minutes
Premiere: August 23, 1933, New York
16 mm Rental: Films Inc.

LITTLE WOMEN (RKO, 1933)
Producer: Merian C. Cooper
Script: Sarah Y. Mason and Victor Heerman. Based on the novel by Louisa
May Alcott and her play *Jo's Boys*
Director of Photography: Henry Gerrard
Editor: Jack Kitchin
Set Designer: Van Nest Polglase
Costumes: Walter Plunkett
Music: Max Steiner
Cast: Katharine Hepburn (Jo), Joan Bennett (Amy), Paul Lukas (Professor
Baer), Frances Dee (Meg), Jean Parker (Beth), Edna May Oliver (Aunt
March), Douglass Montgomery (Laurie), Spring Byington (Marmee)
Running Time: 115 minutes
Premiere: November 1933, New York
16 mm Rental: Films Inc.

DAVID COPPERFIELD (MGM, 1935)
Producer: David O. Selznick
Script: Hugh Walpole and Howard Estabrook. Based on the novel by Charles
Dickens
Director of Photography: Oliver T. Marsh
Editor: Robert J. Kern
Art Directors: Cedric Gibbons, Merrill Pye, Edwin B. Willis
Costumes: Dolly Tree
Music: Herbert Stothart, Charles Maxwell
Cast: W. C. Fields (Micawber), Lionel Barrymore (Dan Peggoty), Edna May
Oliver (Betsey Trotwood), Frank Lawton (David Copperfield as a man),
Freddie Bartholomew (David Copperfield as a boy), Roland Young (Uriah
Heep), Basil Rathbone (Mr. Murdstone)
Running Time: 133 minutes
Premiere: January 1935, New York
16 mm Rental: Films Inc.

SYLVIA SCARLETT (RKO, 1936)
Producer: Pandro S. Berman
Script: Gladys Unger, John Collier, and Mortimer Offner. Based on the novel

by Compton Mackenzie
Director of Photography: Joseph August
Editor: Jane Loring
Art Director: Van Vest Polglase
Costumes: Muriel King, Bernard Newman
Music: Roy Webb
Cast: Katharine Hepburn (Sylvia Scarlett), Cary Grant (Jimmy Monkley),
Brian Aherne (Michael Fane), Edmund Gwenn (Henry Scarlett)
Running Time: 90 minutes
Premiere: January 1936, New York
16 mm Rental: Films Inc.

ROMEO AND JULIET (MGM, 1936)
Producer: Irving Thalberg
Script: Talbot Jennings. Based on the play by William Shakespeare
Director of Photography: William Daniels
Editor: Margaret Booth
Art Directors: Cedric Gibbons, Fredric Hope, Edwin B. Willis, Oliver
Messel
Costumes: Oliver Messel, Adrian
Music: Herbert Stothart (themes by Tchaikovsky)
Choreography: Agnes DeMille
Cast: Norma Shearer (Juliet), Leslie Howard (Romeo), John Barrymore
(Mercutio), Edna May Oliver (Nurse), Basil Rathbone (Tybalt), C. Aubrey
Smith (Lord Capulet)
Running Time: 124 minutes
Premiere: August 1936, New York
16 mm Rental: Films Inc.

CAMILLE (MGM, 1937)
Producer: David Lewis
Script: Zoë Akins, Frances Marion, James Hilton. Based on the novel and
play *La Dame Aux Camelias* by Alexandre Dumas *fils*
Directors of Photography: William Daniels, Karl Freund
Editor: Margaret Booth
Art Directors: Cedric Gibbons, Fredric Hope
Costumes: Adrian
Music: Herbert Stothart
Cast: Greta Garbo (Marguerite Gauthier), Robert Taylor (Armand Duval),
Lionel Barrymore (General Duval), Henry Daniell (Baron de Varville),
Laura Hope Crews (Prudence), Rex O'Malley (Gaston)
Running Time: 108 minutes
Premiere: January 1937, New York
16 mm Rental: Films Inc.

HOLIDAY (Columbia, 1938—British title, FREE TO LIVE or UNCON-
VENTIONAL LINDA)
Producer: Everett Riskin
Script: Donald Ogden Stewart, Sidney Buchman. Based on the play by
Philip Barry
Director of Photography: Franz Planer
Editors: Otto Meyer, Al Clark
Art Directors: Stephen Goosson, Lionel Banks
Costumes: Kalloch
Music: Morris Stoloff
Cast: Katharine Hepburn (Linda Seton), Cary Grant (Johnny Case), Edward
Everett Horton (Nick Potter), Lew Ayres (Ned Seton), Henry Kolker (Ed-
ward Seton)
Running Time: 93 minutes
Premiere: May 1938, New York
16 mm Rental: Audio-Brandon; Images Film Archive

ZAZA (Paramount, 1939)
Producer: Albert Lewin
Script: Zoë Akins. Based on the play by Pierre Berton and Charles Simon
Director of Photography: Charles Lang, Jr.
Editor: Edward Dymtryk
Art Directors: Hans Dreier, Robert Usher
Costumes: Edith Head
Music: Frederick Hollander, Frank Loesser
Cast: Claudette Colbert (Zaza), Herbert Marshall (Dufresne), Bert Lahr
(Cascart), Helen Westley (Anais), Constance Collier (Nathalie)
Running Time: 83 minutes
Premiere: January 1939, New York
16 mm Rental: Swank

THE WOMEN (MGM, 1939)
Producer: Hunt Stromberg
Script: Anita Loos, Jane Murfin (Donald Ogden Stewart, F. Scott Fitzgerald,
uncredited). Based on the play by Clare Boothe
Directors of Photography: Oliver T. Marsh; Joseph Ruttenberg (one se-
quence in Technicolor)
Editor: Robert J. Kern
Art Directors: Cedric Gibbons, Wade B. Rubottom
Costumes: Adrian
Music: Edward Ward, David Snell
Cast: Norma Shearer (Mary Haines), Joan Crawford (Crystal Allen), Rosalind
Russell (Sylvie Fowler), Mary Boland (Countess DeLave), Paulette Goddard

(Miriam Aarons), Joan Fontaine (Peggy Day), Phyliss Povah, Hedda Hopper
Running Time: 134 minutes
Premiere: September 1939, New York
16 mm Rental: Films Inc.

SUSAN AND GOD (MGM, 1940—British title, THE GAY MRS. TREXEL)
Producer: Hunt Stromberg
Script: Anita Loos. Based on the play by Rachel Crothers
Director of Photography: Robert Planck
Editor: William H. Terhune
Art Directors: Cedric Gibbons, Randall Duell, Edwin B. Willis
Music Director: Herbert Stothart
Costumes: Adrian
Cast: Joan Crawford (Susan Trexel), Fredric March (Barry Trexel), Ruth
Hussey (Charlotte), Rita Hayworth (Leonora Stubbs), Nigel Bruce (Hutchins
Stubbs), Marjorie Main (Mary), Constance Collier (Lady Wiggstaff), Dan
Dailey, Jr. (Homer), Gloria De Haven (Enid)
Running Time: 115 minutes
Premiere: June 1940, New York
16 mm Rental: Films Inc.

THE PHILADELPHIA STORY (MGM, 1940)
Producer: Joseph L. Mankiewicz
Script: Donald Ogden Stewart (Waldo Salt, uncredited). Based on the play
by Philip Barry
Director of Photography: Joseph Ruttenberg
Editor: Frank Sullivan
Art Directors: Cedric Gibbons, Wade B. Rubottom
Costumes: Adrian
Music: Franz Waxman
Cast: Katharine Hepburn (Tracy Lord), Cary Grant (C. K. Dexter Haven),
James Stewart (Macauley Connor), Ruth Hussey (Liz Imbrie), John Howard
(George Kittredge), Roland Young (Uncle Willie), John Halliday (Seth Lord)
Running Time: 115 minutes
Premiere: December 1940, New York
16 mm Rental: Films Inc.

A WOMAN'S FACE (MGM, 1941)
Producer: Victor Saville
Script: Donald Ogden Stewart, Elliot Paul (Christopher Isherwood, uncredited). Based on the play *Il etait une fois* by Francis de Croisset and the film *En
kvinnas ansikte* by Gustav Molander

Director of Photography: Robert Planck
Editor: Frank Sullivan
Art Directors: Cedric Gibbons, Wade Rubottom
Costumes: Adrian, Gile Steele
Music: Bronislau Kaper
Cast: Joan Crawford (Anna Holm), Melvyn Douglas (Dr. Segert), Conrad Veidt (Torsten Barring), Reginald Owen (Bernard Dalvik), Doris Day (Girl at Party)
Running Time: 105 minutes
Premiere: May 1941, New York
16 mm Rental: Films Inc.

TWO-FACED WOMAN (MGM, 1941)
Producer: Gottfried Reinhardt
Script: S. N. Behrman, Salka Viertel, George Oppenheimer. Based on the play by Ludwig Fulda
Director of Photography: Joseph Ruttenberg
Editor: George Boemler
Art Directors: Cedric Gibbons, Daniel B. Cathcart
Costumes: Adrian
Music: Bronislau Kaper
Cast: Greta Garbo (Karin/Katrin Borg), Melvyn Douglas (Larry Blake), Constance Bennett (Gliselde Vaughan), Roland Young (Oscar Miller), Ruth Gordon (Ruth Ellis)
Running Time: 85 minutes
Premiere: November 1941, New York
16 mm Rental: Films Inc.

HER CARDBOARD LOVER (MGM, 1942)
Producer: J. Walter Ruben
Script: Jacques Deval, John Collier, Anthony Veiller, William H. Wright. Based on the play by Jacques Deval, adapted by Valerie Wyngate; revised by P. G. Wodehouse
Directors of Photography: Harry Stradling, Robert Planck
Editor: Robert J. Kern
Art Directors: Cedric Gibbons, Randall Duell
Costumes: Kalloch
Music: Franz Waxman
Cast: Norma Shearer (Consuelo Croyden), Robert Taylor (Terry Trindale), George Sanders (Tony Barling), Frank McHugh (Chippie Champagne)
Running Time: 90 minutes
Premiere: July 11, 1942, New York
16 mm Rental: Not available

KEEPER OF THE FLAME (MGM, 1943)
Producer: Victor Saville
Script: Donald Ogden Stewart. Based on the story by I. A. R. Wylie
Director of Photography: William Daniels
Editor: James E. Newcom
Art Directors: Cedric Gibbons, Lyle Wheeler
Costumes: Adrian
Music: Bronislau Kaper
Cast: Spencer Tracy (Stephen O'Malley), Katharine Hepburn (Christine Forrest), Margaret Wycherly (Mrs. Forrest), Percy Kilbride (Orion), Howard Da Silva (Jason Rickards), Horace [later Stephen] McNally (Freddie)
Running Time: 100 minutes
Premiere: January 1943, New York
16 mm Rental: Films Inc.

GASLIGHT (MGM, 1944—British title, MURDER IN THORNTON SQUARE)
Producer: Arthur Hornblow, Jr.
Script: John Van Druten, Walter Reisch, John L. Balderston. Based on the play by Patrick Hamilton
Director of Photography: Joseph Ruttenberg
Editor: Ralph E. Winters
Art Directors: Cedric Gibbons, William Ferrari, Paul Huldchinsky
Costumes: Irene
Music: Bronislau Kaper
Cast: Charles Boyer (Gregory Anton), Ingrid Bergman (Paula Alquist), Joseph Cotten (Brian Cameron), Dame May Whitty (Miss Thwaites), Angela Lansbury (Nancy Oliver)
Running Time: 114 minutes
Premiere: May 1944, New York
16 mm Rental: Films Inc.

WINGED VICTORY (Twentieth Century–Fox)
Producer: Darryl F. Zanuck
Script: Moss Hart. Based on his own play
Director of Photography: Glen MacWilliams
Editor: Barbara McLean
Production Designer: Harry Horner
Costumes: Kay Nelson
Music: David Rose
Cast: Pvt. Lon McCallister (Frankie Davis), Jeanne Crain (Helen), Sgt. Edmund O'Brien (Irving Miller), Cpl. Don Taylor (Danny 'Pinky' Scariano), Cpl. Lee J. Cobb (Doctor), Judy Holliday (Ruth Miller), T/Sgt Peter Lind

Hayes (O'Brian), Cpl. Red Buttons (Whitey), Cpl. Barry Nelson (Bobby
Grills), Cpl. Gary Merrill (Col. Ross), Pvt. Alfred Ryder (Milhauser), Cpl.
Karl Malden (Adams), Pvt. Martin Ritt (Gleason)
Running Time: 130 minutes
Premiere: December 1944, New York
16 mm Rental: Walter Reade; Films Inc.

A DOUBLE LIFE (Universal–International, 1947)
Producer: Michael Kanin
Script: Ruth Gordon, Garson Kanin
Director of Photography: Milton Krasner
Editor: Robert Parrish
Art Directors: Bernard Herzbrun, Harvey Gillett
Costumes: Travis Banton, Yvonne Wood
Music: Miklos Rozsa
Technical Adviser for the *Othello* sequence: Walter Hampden
Cast: Ronald Colman (Anthony John), Signe Hasso (Brita), Edmond O'Brien
(Bill Friend), Shelley Winters (Pat Kroll), Ray Collins (Victor Donlan), Philip
Loeb (Max Lasker), John Drew Colt (Stage Manager), Betsy Blair (Girl in wig
shop), Paddy Chayefsky (Photographer), John Derek (Police stenographer),
Elmo Lincoln (Detective)
Running Time: 105 minutes
Premiere: December 1947, New York
16 mm Rental: Kit Parker; Ivy

EDWARD, MY SON (MGM, 1949)
Producer: Edwin H. Knopf
Script: Donald Ogden Stewart. Based on the play by Robert Morley and Noel
Langley
Director of Photography: Freddie Young
Editor: Raymond Poulton
Art Director: Albert Junge
Music: John Wooldridge
Cast: Spencer Tracy (Arnold Boult), Deborah Kerr (Evelyn Boult), Ian
Hunter (Dr. Larry Woodhope), Leueen MacGrath (Eileen Perrin), Felix
Aylmer (Mr. Hanray)
Running Time: 112 minutes
Premiere: March 4, 1949, London
16 mm Rental: Films Inc.

ADAM'S RIB (MGM, 1949)
Producer: Lawrence Weingarten
Script: Ruth Gordon, Garson Kanin

Director of Photography: George Folsey
Editor: George Boemler
Art Directors: Cedric Gibbons, William Ferrari, Henry W. Grace
Music: Miklos Rozsa; Cole Porter
Costumes: Walter Plunkett
Cast: Spencer Tracy (Adam Bonner), Katharine Hepburn (Amanda Bonner), Judy Holliday (Doris Attinger), Tom Ewell (Warren Attinger), David Wayne (Kip Lurie), Jean Hagen (Beryl Caighn), Polly Moran (Mrs. McGrath), Anna Q. Nilsson (Mrs. Poynter)
Running Time: 101 minutes
Premiere: November 1949, New York
16 mm Rental: Films Inc. Also available on videocassette

A LIFE OF HER OWN (MGM, 1950)
Producer: Voldemar Vetluguin
Script: Isobel Lennart
Director of Photography: George Folsey
Editor: George White
Art Directors: Cedric Gibbons, Arthur Lonergan
Music: Bronislau Kaper
Cast: Lana Turner (Lily Brannel James), Ray Milland (Steve Harleigh), Tom Ewell (Tom Caraway), Louis Calhern (Jim Leversoe), Ann Dvorak (Mary Ashlon), Hermes Pan (Lily's dance partner)
Running Time: 150 minutes; cut to 108 minutes
Premiere: August 1950, New York
16 mm Rental: Films Inc.

BORN YESTERDAY (Columbia, 1950)
Producer: S. Sylvan Simon
Script: Albert Mannheimer (Garson Kanin, uncredited). Based on the play by Garson Kanin
Director of Photography: Joseph Walker
Editor: Charles Nelson
Music: Frederick Hollander
Production Designer: Harry Horner
Cast: Judy Holliday (Billie Dawn), Broderick Crawford (Harry Brock), William Holden (Paul Verrall), Howard St. John (Jim Devery), Frank Otto (Eddie)
Running Time: 102 minutes
Premiere: November 1950, New York
16 mm Rental: Audio-Brandon; Images Film Archive. Also available on videocassette

THE MODEL AND THE MARRIAGE BROKER (Twentieth Century–
Fox, 1951)
Producer: Charles Brackett
Script: Charles Brackett, Walter Reisch, Richard Breen, James Vincent
Director of Photography: Milton Krasner
Editor: Robert Simpson
Art Directors: Lyle Wheeler, John De Cuir
Music: Cyril Mockridge
Costumes: Renie
Cast: Jeannie Crain (Kitty), Scott Brady (Matt), Thelma Ritter (Mae Swazey),
Zero Mostel (Wixted), Michael O'Shea (Doberman), Frank Fontaine
(Johannson), Mae Marsh (Woman)
Running Time: 103 minutes
Premiere: November 1951, New York
16 mm Rental: Films Inc.

THE MARRYING KIND (Columbia, 1952)
Producer: Bert Granet
Script: Ruth Gordon, Garson Kanin
Director of Photography: Joseph Walker
Editor: Ralph Nelson
Art Director: John Meehan
Costumes: Jean Louis
Music: Hugo Friedhofer
Cast: Judy Holliday (Florence Keefer), Aldo Ray (Chet Keefer), Madge
Kennedy (Judge Anna Carroll), Peggy Cass (Emily Bundy), Charles
Buchinski [later Bronson] (Eddie)
Running Time: 93 minutes
Premiere: March 1952, New York
16 mm Rental: Audio-Brandon

PAT AND MIKE (MGM, 1952)
Producer: Lawrence Weingarten
Script: Ruth Gordon, Garson Kanin
Director of Photography: William Daniels
Editor: George Boemier
Costumes for Ms. Hepburn: Orry-Kelly
Art Directors: Cedric Gibbons, Urie McCleary
Music: David Raksin
Cast: Spencer Tracy (Mike Conovan), Katharine Hepburn (Pat Pemberton),
Aldo Ray (Davie Hucko); Gussie Moran, Babe Didrikson Zaharias, Don
Budge, Alice Marble, Frank Parker, Betty Hicks, Beverly Hanson, Helen
Dettweiler as themselves; Chuck Connors (Police Captain), Mae Clark

(Woman Golfer)
Running Time: 95 minutes
Premiere: June 1952, New York
16 mm Rental: Films Inc.

THE ACTRESS (MGM, 1953)
Producer: Lawrence Weingarten
Script: Ruth Gordon. Based on her play *Years Ago*
Director of Photography: Harold Rosson
Editor: George Boemler
Art Directors: Cedric Gibbons, Arthur Lonergan
Music: Bronislau Kaper
Costumes: Walter Plunkett
Cast: Spencer Tracy (Clinton Jones), Jean Simmons (Ruth Gordon Jones), Teresa Wright (Annie Jones), Anthony Perkins (Fred Whitmarsh), Jackie Coogan (Man Heckler)
Running Time: 90 minutes
Premiere: June 1953, New York
16 mm Rental: Films Inc.

IT SHOULD HAPPEN TO YOU (Columbia, 1954)
Producer: Fred Kohlmar
Script: Garson Kanin
Director of Photography: Charles Lang
Editor: Charles Nelson
Art Director: John Meehan
Music: Frederick Hollander
Costumes: Jean Louis
Cast: Judy Holliday (Gladys Glover), Peter Lawford (Evan Adams III), Jack Lemmon (Pete Sheppard), Michael O'Shea (Brod Clinton); Ilka Chase, Constance Bennett, Wendy Barrie as themselves
Running Time: 87 minutes
Premiere: March 1954, New York
16 mm Rental: Twyman

A STAR IS BORN (Warner Bros., 1954)
Producer: Sidney Luft
Script: Moss Hart. Based on the screenplay by Dorothy Parker, Alan Campbell, and Robert Carson for the film *A Star Is Born* (1937). Inspired by the screenplay by Gene Fowler and Rowland Brown for the film *What Price Hollywood?* (1932).
Director of Photography: Sam Leavitt (CinemaScope, Technicolor)

Editor: Folmar Blangsted
Production Designer: Gene Allen
Music: Harold Arlen, Leonard Gershe
Costumes: Jean Louis, Mary Ann Nyberg, Irene Sharaff
Cast: Judy Garland (Esther Blodgett, later Vicki Lester), James Mason
(Norman Maine), Jack Carson (Matt Libby), Charles Bickford (Oliver Niles),
Tommy Noonan (Danny McGuire)
Running Time: 182 minutes; cut to 154 minutes
Premiere: October 1954, New York
16 mm Rental: Audio-Brandon

BHOWANI JUNCTION (MGM, 1956)
Producer: Pandro S. Berman
Script: Sonya Levien, Ivan Moffat. Based on the novel by John Masters
Director of Photography: Freddie Young (CinemaScope, Eastman Color)
Editors: Frank Clarke, George Boemler
Art Directors: Gene Allen, John Howell
Costumes: Elizabeth Haffenden
Music: Miklos Rozsa
Cast: Ava Gardner (Victoria Jones), Stewart Granger (Colonel Rodney Savage), Bill Travers (Patrick Taylor), Abraham Sofaer (Surabhai)
Running Time: 110 minutes
Premiere: May 1956, New York
16 mm Rental: Films Inc.

LES GIRLS (MGM, 1957)
Producer: Sol C. Siegel
Script: John Patrick. Based on a story by Vera Caspary
Director of Photography: Robert Surtees (CinemaScope, Metrocolor)
Editor: Ferris Webster
Art Directors: William A. Horning, Gene Allen
Costumes: Orry-Kelly
Music: Cole Porter
Cast: Gene Kelly (Barry Nichols), Kay Kendall (Lady Sybil Wren), Mitzi
Gaynor (Joy Henderson), Taina Elg (Angele Ducros), Jacques Bergerac
(Pierre Ducros)
Running Time: 114 minutes
Premiere: October 1957, New York
16 mm Rental: Films Inc.

WILD IS THE WIND (Paramount, 1957)
Producer: Hal B. Wallis
Script: Arnold Schulman. Based on a scenario by Vittorio Nino Novarese and

the film *Furia* (1946) directed by Goffredo Alessandrini
Director of Photography: Charles Lang, Jr. (VistaVision)
Editor: Warren Low
Art Directors: Hal Pereira, Tambi Larsen
Music: Dimitri Tiomkin
Costumes: Edith Head
Cast: Anna Magnani (Gioia), Anthony Quinn (Gino), Anthony Franciosa (Bene), Dolores Hart (Angie), Joseph Calleia (Alberto)
Running Time: 114 minutes
Premiere: December 1957, New York
16 mm Rental: Audio-Brandon

HELLER IN PINK TIGHTS (Paramount, 1960)
Producer: Carlo Ponti
Script: Dudley Nichols, Walter Bernstein. Based on the novel *Heller with a Gun* by Louis L'Amour
Director of Photography: Harold Lipstein (Technicolor)
Editor: Howard Smith
Art Director: Gene Allen
Costumes: Edith Head
Music: Daniele Amfitheatrof
Cast: Sophia Loren (Angela Rossini), Anthony Quinn (Tom Healy), Margaret O'Brien (Della Southby), Steve Forrest (Clint Mabry), Eileen Heckart (Mrs. Lorna Hathaway), Ramon Novarro (DeLeon), Edmund Lowe (Manfred "Doc" Montague)
Running Time: 100 minutes
Premiere: March 1960, New York
16 mm Rental: Audio-Brandon

LET'S MAKE LOVE (Twentieth Century–Fox, 1960)
Producer: Jerry Wald
Script: Norman Krasna, Hal Kanter
Director of Photography: Daniel L. Fapp (CinemaScope, Color by DeLuxe)
Editor: David Bretherton
Art Directors: Lyle R. Wheeler, Gene Allen
Music: Lionel Newman, Earle H. Hagen; Sammy Cahn; Cole Porter
Costumes: Dorothy Jeakins
Cast: Marilyn Monroe (Amanda Dell), Yves Montand (Jean-Marc Clement), Tony Randall (Alex Coffman), Wilfrid Hyde-White (George Wales); Gene Kelly, Bing Crosby, Milton Berle as themselves
Running Time: 118 minutes
Premiere: September 1960, New York
16 mm Rental: Films Inc.

THE CHAPMAN REPORT (Warner Bros., 1962)
Producer: Richard D. Zanuck
Script: Wyatt Cooper, Don M. Mankiewicz, Arthur Sheekman, Grant
Stuart, Gene Allen. Based on the novel by Irving Wallace
Director of Photography: Harold Lipstein (Technicolor)
Editor: Robert Simpson
Production Designer: Gene Allen
Music: Leonard Rosenman
Costumes: Orry-Kelly
Cast: Efrem Zimbalist, Jr. (Paul Radford), Shelley Winters (Sarah Garnell),
Jane Fonda (Kathleen Barclay), Claire Bloom (Naomi Shields), Glynis Johns
(Teresa Harnish), Andrew Duggan (Dr. George C. Chapman)
Running Time: 132 minutes; cut to 125 minutes
Premiere: October 1962, New York
16 mm Rental: Warner Bros., Twyman

MY FAIR LADY (Warner Bros., 1964)
Producer: Jack L. Warner
Script: Alan Jay Lerner. Adapted from his musical play, based on George
Bernard Shaw's play *Pygmalion* and on Shaw's screenplay for the film *Pyg-
malion* (1938)
Director of Photography: Harry Stradling (SuperPanavisio⌐ 70, Technicolor)
Editor: William Ziegler
Production Designer: Cecil Beaton
Music: Frederick Loewe, with lyrics by Alan Jay Lerner
Costumes: Cecil Beaton
Art Director: Gene Allen
Cast: Audrey Hepburn (Eliza Doolittle), Rex Harrison (Henry Higgins),
Stanley Holloway (Alfred P. Doolittle), Wilfrid Hyde-White (Colonel Hugh
Pickering), Gladys Cooper (Mrs. Higgins), Jeremy Brett (Freddy
Eynsford-Hill). Miss Hepburn's songs dubbed by Marnie Nixon.
Running Time: 170 minutes
Premiere: October 1964, New York
16 mm Rental: Swank

JUSTINE (Twentieth Century–Fox, 1969)
Producer: Pandro S. Berman
Uncredited Director: Joseph Strick (replaced by Cukor)
Script: Lawrence B. Marcus. Based on *The Alexandria Quartet* by Lawrence
Durrell
Director of Photography: Leon Shamroy (Panavision, Color by DeLuxe)
Editor: Rita Roland

Art Directors: Jack Martin Smith, William Creber
Costumes: Irene Sharaff
Music: Jerry Goldsmith
Cast: Anouk Aimée (Justine), Dirk Bogarde (Pursewarden), Anna Karina (Melissa), Philippe Noiret (Pombal), Michael York (Darley), Jack Albertson (Cohen), Cliff Gorman (Toto), Marcel Dalio (French Consul General), Michael Dunn (Mnemjian)
Running Time: 116 minutes
Premiere: August 1969, New York
16 mm Rental: Films Inc.

TRAVELS WITH MY AUNT (MGM, 1972)
Producers: Robert Fryer, James Cresson
Script: Jay Presson Allen, Hugh Wheeler. Based on the novel by Graham Greene
Director of Photography: Douglas Slocombe (Panavision, Metrocolor)
Editor: John Bloom
Production Designer: John Box
Music: Tony Hatch
Costumes: Anthony Powell
Cast: Maggie Smith (Aunt Augusta), Alex McCowen (Henry Pulling), Lou Gossett (Wordsworth), Robert Stephens (Visconti), Cindy Williams (Tooley)
Running Time: 109 minutes
Premiere: December 1972, New York
16 mm Rental: Films Inc.

THE BLUEBIRD (Twentieth Century–Fox/Lenfilm, 1976)
Producers: Paul Maslansky, Alexander Archansky
Script: Alexei Kapler, Hugh Whitmore. Based on the play by Maurice Maeterlinck
Directors of Photography: Jonas Gritsus, Freddie Young (Color)
Editors: Tatiana Shapiro, Ernest Walter
Art Director: Valery Jurkevitch
Music: Andrei Petrov
Costumes: Mariana Azizian, Edith Head
Cast: Elizabeth Taylor (Mother/Maternal Love/Witch/Light), Nadia Pavlova (The Bluebird), Jane Fonda (Night), Ava Gardner (Luxury), Cicely Tyson (Cat), Patsy Kensit (Mytyl), Todd Lookinland (Tyltyl)
Running Time: 99 minutes
Premiere: May 1976, New York
16 mm Rental: Films Inc.

RICH AND FAMOUS (MGM, 1981)
Producer: William Allyn
Script: Gerald Ayres. Suggested by the play *Old Acquaintance* by John Van
Druten
Editor: John F. Burnett
Directors of Photography: Don Peterman; Peter Eco (New York) (Color)
Music: George Delerue
Production Designer: Jan Scott
Art Directors: Fred Harpman; James A. Taylor (New York)
Costumes: Theoni V. Aldredge
Cast: Jacqueline Bisset (Liz), Candice Bergen (Merry), David Selby (Doug),
Hart Bochner (Chris), Meg Ryan (Debby), and Dick Cavett and Merv Griffin
as themselves.
Running Time: 117 minutes
Premiere: October 9, 1981
16mm Rental: Films Inc.

2. *Television Films*

LOVE AMONG THE RUINS (ABC-TV, 1975)
Cast: Katharine Hepburn (Jessica Medlicott), Laurence Olivier (Sir Arthur
Granville-Jones), Colin Blakely (J. F. Devine)

THE CORN IS GREEN (CBS-TV, 1979)
Cast: Katharine Hepburn (Lily C. Moffat), Ian Saynor (Morgan Evans), Anna
Massey (Miss Ronberry)

3. *Marginal Films*
Cukor directed part of the following films without receiving screen credit:

THE ANIMAL KINGDOM (RKO, 1932)
Director: Edward H. Griffith

NO MORE LADIES (MGM, 1935)
Director: Edward H. Griffith

I MET MY LOVE AGAIN (United Artists, 1938)
Directors: Arthur Ripley, Joshua Logan

GONE WITH THE WIND (MGM, 1939)
Director: Victor Fleming (Sam Wood, also uncredited)

I'LL BE SEEING YOU (Selznick International, 1945)
Director: William Dieterle

DESIRE ME (MGM, 1947)
Director: None listed (Mervyn LeRoy, Jack Conway, also uncredited)

MILLION DOLLAR MERMAID (MGM, 1952)
Director: Mervyn LeRoy

HOT SPELL (Paramount, 1958)
Director: Daniel Mann

SONG WITHOUT END (Columbia, 1960)
Director: Charles Vidor

4. Unfinished Work

SOMETHING'S GOT TO GIVE (1962)
Cukor directed this film for three weeks until production was halted when
Marilyn Monroe was not able to complete the picture.

Index